Become A Government Contracting
Wizard

Mastering NDAs for Government Contractors

TIM MAGNUSSON, CPCM

Copyright © 2025 TIM MAGNUSSON, CPCM

All rights reserved.

www.contractsclassroom.com

Available in these formats:
- 979-8-218-95850-3 (eBook)
- 979-8-218-96937-0 (Paperback)

This book is intended to provide accurate information with regard to a specific topic pertaining to Government Contracting. However, ensuring all the information provided is entirely accurate and up-to-date at all times is not always possible. Therefore, the author and publisher accept no responsibility for inaccuracies or omissions and specifically disclaim any liability, loss or risk, personal, professional, or otherwise, which may be incurred as a consequence, directly or indirectly, of the use and/or application of any of the contents of this book.

No part of this book may be reproduced, stored in a retrieval system, or transmitted in any form or by any means, electronic, mechanical, photocopying, recording, or otherwise, without the prior written permission of the publisher, except for brief quotations embodied in critical articles and reviews.

DISCLAIMER: The content of this book should not be considered legal advice. The content was not prepared by an attorney. It is recommended that all legal matters be discussed with an attorney of your choice.

Foreword

For many contracting professionals, NDAs are an intimidating, or underestimated aspect of the contracting process.

Through the pages of this book, I am going to take you on a transformative journey that will revolutionize the way you approach NDAs. Whether you're just starting in the field of government contracting or looking to deepen your expertise, this book is designed to equip you with all the tools, strategies, and insights you need to not only protect your company's interests but also advance your personal career by developing a reputation as a wizard in the contracting profession.

The timing couldn't be more crucial. As the contracting landscape grows increasingly more complex, understanding how to design, negotiate, and create enforceable NDAs is no longer optional — it's a strategic necessity.

This book dives deep into the common clauses of NDAs. In addition, this book offers practical guidance and helpful tips on how to write the clause so that it benefits your situation. I'll explain why each clause is important and how it safeguards your interests. I will provide you with clear examples of each clause and the suggested text you can use in real-world situations. You'll learn not just what to look for, but how to tailor agreements to meet your specific needs and mitigate risks effectively.

With clear explanations, practical examples, and step-by-step strategies, this book transforms NDAs from an administrative hurdle into a powerful tool for success in government contracting. You'll discover how to navigate complex clauses with confidence and position yourself as a trusted expert in the field.

By the time you finish this book, you will have gained the confidence, knowledge, and skills necessary to navigate NDAs with ease. No longer will you feel intimidated or uncertain when reviewing or negotiating an NDA. Instead, you'll feel empowered, capable, and ready to take control of the process with the authority of someone who truly understands the intricacies of these critical documents.

The goal of this book is simple: to transform you from someone who sees NDAs as intimidating legal documents that have to be signed, to becoming your organization's go-to authority on protecting confidential information. By the final chapter, you'll transition from seeking guidance from others to confidently leading NDA strategy and negotiations and confidently declaring, "I am the NDA Wizard." This isn't just about understanding the basics — it's about mastering the art of NDAs to the point where you become an expert.

This is your guide to becoming the NDA Wizard, a trusted professional who understands how to protect what matters most while fostering collaboration in the competitive world of government contracting. Together, let's turn your uncertainty into expertise, your questions into strategies, and your potential into mastery!

Preface

The purpose of *"Become a Government Contracting Wizard: Mastering NDAs for Government Contractors"* is to provide government contracting professionals, and owners of Government Contracting firms, with a comprehensive step-by-step, practical guide to efficiently and effectively review, negotiate, and manage Non-Disclosure Agreements (NDAs).

This book is designed to address two key challenges faced by Government Contractors:

1. **The Misunderstanding of NDAs as "Standard" Documents**:
   Many people involved in the management or execution of government contracts, view NDAs as boilerplate agreements that require minimal attention. This mindset often results in overlooked risks, enforceability issues, and missed opportunities to protect proprietary information. By breaking down the components of an NDA, this book demonstrates how each clause serves a specific purpose and why careful negotiation is essential.

2. **The Need for Efficiency and Expertise**:
   Federal government contracting demands precision, speed, and compliance. A poorly managed NDA can delay teaming agreements, subcontractor relationships, and critical collaborations. This book equips readers with tools, strategies, and insights to streamline NDA workflows while mitigating risk.

Who is This Book For?

This book serves three primary audiences:

1. **Experienced Government Contracting Professionals**
   For professionals who regularly handle NDAs, this book provides advanced insights into:
   - Efficiently negotiating critical NDA terms to save time.
   - Identifying and addressing hidden risks in NDAs.
   - Aligning NDA terms with perceived risk and corporate policy.
   - Implementing tools and best practices to manage NDAs across their lifecycle.
2. **New Professionals or Transitioning Contract Managers**
   For individuals new to the field, such as recent graduates or professionals transitioning from other industries, this book serves as a foundational guide by:
   - Explaining the basics of NDAs in clear and accessible language.
   - Providing real-world examples, templates, and checklists to build confidence.
   - Highlighting the importance of NDAs in the broader federal contracting process.
3. **Owners of Government Contracting Small Businesses**
   For those small business owners that must share critical information without fear of exploitation, this book offers a bridge to success by:
   - Explaining how NDAs can ensure their competitive advantage remains intact.
   - Explaining the content of clauses, and their intent, in everyday language.
   - Providing a step-by-step approach to reviewing, negotiating, and managing NDAs effectively.
   - Highlighting common pitfalls and risks specific to government contracts and partnerships.

By addressing the needs of all experience levels, this book ensures that every reader can become a **NDA Wizard**.

What This Book Offers

This book bridges the gap between theory and practical application. It has been designed as both a **step-by-step guide** and a **quick reference resource**. By reading each chapter in sequence, the reader can build a solid understanding of NDAs. The checklist, templates, and sample clauses allow the reader to address specific challenges during review or negotiation. Specifically, this book provides the reader:

- **Clause-by-Clause Analysis**: Detailed explanations of the intent of each clause, including its purpose, associated risks, examples of industry-standard language, and common companion clauses.
- **Risk Management and Compliance**: Strategies for balancing risks and responsibilities while maintaining strong relationships with partners and understanding how to strike the right balance between protection and practicality.
- **Negotiation Strategies**: Techniques for negotiating fair, balanced, and enforceable NDA terms that ensure both parties' interests are protected while maintaining a practical and effective agreement.
- **Best Practices**: Practical guidance for implementing standardized workflows, leveraging technology, and monitoring NDA compliance.
- **Build Confidence and Efficiency**: Templates and Checklists to reduce review time and improve negotiation outcomes.

Whether you are an experienced contracting professional looking to fine-tune your NDA processes or a new contracting professional building foundational skills, this book provides the tools and knowledge you need to **"become a wizard"** at managing NDAs in federal contracting.

Let's get started on your journey to mastering NDAs!

Contents

Part I: Foundations of NDAs in Government Contracting

Chapter 1: What is a NDA and Why It Matters 1
- What is a Non-Disclosure Agreement? 1
- The Critical Role of NDAs in Government Contracting 2
- When Do You Need an NDA? 3
- Misconceptions About NDAs 4
- Conclusion 7

Chapter 2: The Basics 9
- Common Names for NDAs 9
- Most Common Uses of NDAs 10
- Types of NDAs 11
- Key Functions of NDAs 11
- When are NDAs Required for Government Contractors? 12
- Structure and Length of NDAs 13
- The Importance of Due Diligence 14
- Avoiding Common NDA Pitfalls 14
- When a NDA May Not Be Necessary 15

Chapter 3: Key Players and Stakeholders 16
- Internal Stakeholders 16
- External Stakeholders 18
- Why Stakeholder Coordination is Critical 19
- Conclusion 20

Part II: Dissecting and Mastering NDA Clauses 21

Chapter 4: Dissecting and Mastering NDA Clauses 22
   Introduction 22
   LEGAL NAMES OF ALL PARTIES 26
   DEFINITIONS 29
   EFFECTIVE DATE 34
   SPECIFIC PURPOSE 38
   RECIPENT OBLIGATIONS 42
   COVERED INFORMATION 47
   INFORMATION EXCLUDED FROM PROTECTION 54
   STANDARDS OF CARE 59
   PERMITTED DISCLOSURE 65
   NOTICE OF BREACH 71
   CHOICE OF LAW 76
   NO IMPLIED LICENSE 86
   TERM or DURATION PERIOD 90
   PROTECTION PERIOD 94
   AFFILIATES AND THIRD PARTIES 99
   RESTRICTED USE 105
   RIGHTS IN DATA 111
   REMEDIES FOR BREACH 118
   ALTERNATIVE DISPUTE RESOLUTIONS 122
   RETURN OF PROPRIETARY INFORMATION 135
   ASSIGNMENT 142
   CHANGE OF CONTROL OR OWNERSHIP 149
   IMPORT & EXPORT RESTRICTIONS 156

    TERMINATION 160

    WARRANTIES...166

    LIQUIDATED DAMAGES...172

    RESPONSIBLE PARTIES 177

    SEVERABLE...182

    SURVIVABLE TERMS 186

    ENTIRE AGREEMENT 195

Part III: Negotiation and Management 199

Chapter 5: Negotiation Strategies 200

    Why Clauses Matter 201

    Key Themes in Negotiation...201

    Prioritize Key Clauses 202

    Acknowledge Red Flags...203

    A Strategic Approach to Negotiation 203

    Use a Collaborative Approach 204

    Be Prepared to Justify Your Position 204

    Leverage Companion Clauses 204

    Avoid Boilerplate Overuse 205

    Know When to Escalate 205

    Use Real-World Examples to Build Consensus 206

    Document and Track Negotiation Changes........................206

    Plan for Long-Term Success 206

    Putting Knowledge Into Action...207

    Conclusion 207

Chapter 6: Avoiding Overreach 209

    What is Overreach in NDAs?..209

    Why Overreach is Problematic..210

    Recognizing Signs of Overreach..211

    Balancing Protection and Practicality 212

    Conclusion...213

Chapter 7: Common Pitfalls 214

    Vague or Overbroad Definitions of Confidential Information...........214

    Missing or Unrealistic Term or Duration 215

    Failure to Address Permitted Disclosures 216

    Overly Restrictive Permitted Use..217

    Neglecting Remedies for Breach...217

    Ignoring Choice of Law and Jurisdiction 218

    Overreaching Obligations to Affiliates and Subcontractors...............218

    Conclusion...219

Chapter 8: Compliance and Enforcement...................................220

    Introduction 220

    Compliance: The Responsibility of the Receiving Party...................220

    Establishing Clear Procedures:..220

    The Importance of Record-Keeping for Enforcement.......................221

    Enforcing an NDA: Steps and Options for the Disclosing Party........222

    Enforcement Pathways..223

    Consequences of Violating an NDA 224

    Compliance and Enforcement: Prime Contractors vs. Subcontractors
   225

    Conclusion...225

Chapter 9: System Management **227**
    Introduction 227
    Develop a Standardized NDA Process 229
    Leverage Technology for NDA Management 230
    Train Teams on NDA Policies and Responsibilities 230
    Monitor and Enforce NDA Obligations 231
    Avoid Overuse of NDAs 232
    Maintain NDA Visibility Across the Contract Lifecycle 232
    Lessons Learned and Continuous Improvement 233
    Conclusion 233

Appendix 1: NDA Review Checklist **235**

Appendix 2: Due Diligence Checklist **239**

Appendix 3: Template for NDA **245**

Afterword **263**

About the Author **265**

Part I
Foundations of NDAs in Federal Government Contracting

Chapter 1
What is a NDA and Why It Matters

Introduction

Non-Disclosure Agreements (NDAs) are the bedrock of trust in government contracts. These agreements ensure that proprietary or sensitive information remains protected throughout business negotiations, teaming agreements or arrangements, and contract performance. Despite their importance, NDAs are often treated as routine, "standard" documents, leading to rushed cursory reviews, overlooked clauses, and unnecessary risks.

What is a Non-Disclosure Agreement?

A Non-Disclosure Agreement (NDA) is a legally binding contract in which one or more parties agree to maintain the confidentiality of certain information. It serves to define what information is protected, who is obligated to protect it, how the information can be used, and the duration of confidentiality obligations. This includes not exposing the information to unauthorized third parties and also promising not to use it without the disclosing party's permission.

At its core, a NDA should contain 6 basic provisions:

1. **What information is protected** (referred to as Proprietary or *Confidential Information*).

2. **Who is bound** to protect the information (the Disclosing and *Receiving Parties*).

3. **Permitted purposes** for which the information can be used.

4. **The duration** for which the confidentiality obligation applies.

5. **Information that is excluded** from the protections of the NDA.

6. **Consequences and legal remedies** in the event of a breach.

The Critical Role of NDAs in Government Contracting

Safeguarding Proprietary and Sensitive Information

In the competitive landscape of government contracting, where contractors often serve as both rivals and teaming partners, collaborating with the competition becomes a necessary step to achieve growth, expand capabilities, and enhance past performance.

In such an environment, protecting your firm's sensitive, proprietary, or confidential information is a top priority. Equally important is demonstrating to your "friendly competitors" that you have the systems, processes, and safeguards in place to protect their data with the same diligence you apply to your own.

This delicate "frenemy" relationship between contractors depends on trust, efficiency, and mutual understanding. Given this complex dynamic, NDAs play a vital role by providing assurance that shared information will be protected. NDAs enable open collaboration in teaming agreements, subcontractor relationships, and joint ventures. This trust fosters smoother negotiations and stronger partnerships.

When Do You Need an NDA?

NDAs are only necessary when the Disclosing Party requires the Receiving Party to promise not to share proprietary information or company sensitive information with any unauthorized individuals, or companies, during the contracting process. The party that is receiving the confidential information ("Receiving Party") agrees to be limited and bound by obligations of confidentiality in exchange for any potential benefit that he or she might receive from the Disclosing Party. This could include a profitable licensing partnership, a job offer, collaboration on a proposal, or the potential possibility of purchasing the Disclosing Party's business.

NDAs are not required by any Federal Contracting Regulation. The use of a NDA is purely a business decision. Common scenarios that encourage the use of NDAs include:

- **Teaming Agreements**: When partners collaborate to pursue contract opportunities and share proprietary bid, or proposal, strategies.

- **Subcontracting Relationships**: When prime contractors disclose technical or pricing data to subcontractors.

- **Proposal Preparation**: When parties negotiate sensitive terms, pricing structures, or deliverables as part of a contract proposal.

- **Technology Sharing**: When innovations, patents, or Controlled Unclassified Information (CUI) are shared for research, development, or operational purposes.

- **Vendor Engagement**: When vendors receive confidential details to provide services or deliver solutions.

Each of these scenarios suggests the need for a tailored NDA to reflect the sensitivity of the data being shared and the responsibilities of the receiving party.

Misconceptions About NDAs

NDAs are often misunderstood or underestimated in their complexity and importance. Many government contracting professionals think of NDAs as straight forward "boilerplate" documents that require minimal review. However, this mindset can lead to critical oversights, unenforceable agreements, and unnecessary risks. To properly approach NDAs, it is important to address some of the most common misconceptions and understand why they are dangerous to the integrity of any business relationship.

"It's Just Boilerplate"

One of the most prevalent misconceptions about NDAs is the belief that they are "just boilerplate"—standardized, generic agreements that can be reused across different projects or relationships, and because they are generic, "boilerplate" agreements, no more than a minimal review is required. While certain clauses may appear similar, NDAs are highly context-specific and must be tailored to address the unique circumstances of each contract, solicitation, or engagement.

The nature of the relationship, the type of confidential information being shared, and the regulatory environment all influence the terms of the NDA. For example, a teaming agreement between two prime contractors requires a far more robust NDA than a simple subcontractor relationship, as both parties may be sharing proprietary technical information, pricing strategies, and sensitive bid data. Similarly, data shared on defense contracts or involving Controlled Unclassified Information (CUI) triggers specific regulatory obligations under FAR, DFARS, or export control laws, such as ITAR or EAR. A generic NDA may fail to meet these requirements, exposing the parties to significant compliance risks.

Another issue with treating NDAs as boilerplate is ambiguity. Overly broad or poorly defined terms can create confusion about what is protected, or allowed, under the agreement. For instance, vague definitions of "Confidential Information" could lead to disputes over whether certain data qualifies for protection. Courts may refuse to enforce such agreements, leaving sensitive information unprotected and rendering the NDA meaningless.

NDAs must be carefully reviewed and customized to reflect the scope of the engagement, the sensitivity of the data, and the operational requirements of the parties involved. Viewing a NDA as a "one-size-fits-all" document increases the risk of ambiguity, noncompliance, and unintended liability. Treating it as a tailored, strategic tool ensures that it achieves its purpose effectively.

"NDAs Are Always Mutual"

Another common assumption is that NDAs must always be mutual, where both parties share confidential information under identical obligations. While mutual NDAs are appropriate for partnerships or joint ventures where both parties exchange sensitive data, many relationships require only a one-sided (unilateral) NDA.

Mutual NDAs often create unnecessary obligations for the receiving party when no information of equal value is being exchanged. For example, in a subcontractor relationship, the prime contractor may be the sole party sharing proprietary data. In this case, a mutual NDA would unnecessarily impose obligations on the subcontractor. Similarly, assuming equal risk in a mutual NDA can create imbalanced protections and lead to unnecessary negotiations.

A mutual NDA can also create the false impression that both parties share equal liability and risk. In reality, one party may have far more sensitive information at stake. Asymmetrical risks require NDAs that reflect the flow of information rather than impose unnecessary obligations. When mutual NDAs are used without thought, they may contain terms that one party cannot reasonably comply with, leading to friction or delays.

This does not mean mutual NDAs are never appropriate. In relationships where both parties are sharing proprietary data, mutual NDAs create balance and protection. Similarly, it is not totally uncommon that multiple parties must execute the same NDA (multilateral) in order to promote equal and efficient communications among multiple parties. However, the obligations must still be fair, proportional, and reflective of each party's actual risk. Professionals must evaluate the flow of information in each relationship to determine whether a mutual, a multilateral, or an unilateral NDA is appropriate. Mutual agreements should only be used when both parties genuinely share sensitive data and require equal protections.

"Once Signed, We're Safe"

A particularly dangerous misconception is the idea that once a NDA is signed, the work is done and the parties are protected. Signing a NDA is only the first step. The real work begins with ensuring ongoing compliance, monitoring obligations, and implementing procedures to prevent unauthorized disclosures.

An NDA, no matter how well written, cannot enforce itself. For the agreement to be effective, internal teams, subcontractors, and vendors must be aware of their obligations and responsibilities. Without proper training and communication, breaches can occur unintentionally. For example, a program team unfamiliar with the NDA's permitted use clause might share proprietary data with a consultant (a third party) without realizing they are violating the agreement. Similarly, failing to establish standards of care for handling confidential data—such as encrypting sensitive files or limiting access—can lead to unintentional misuse or loss.

Compliance with NDA obligations must be ongoing. Organizations must employ monitoring mechanisms to ensure that confidentiality terms are being met. Tools such as contract management software can help track obligations, remind teams of key milestones (e.g., returning or destroying data), and ensure that critical deadlines are not missed.

Another common oversight occurs at the end of an NDA's lifecycle. Many NDAs include clauses requiring the return or destruction of confidential information once the relationship ends, but these obligations are often neglected. If data is not properly disposed of, the disclosing party's sensitive information remains at risk, and the receiving party may be in breach of the agreement.

To address this, organizations should establish formal protocols for monitoring and enforcing NDA terms. These include training teams on the importance of confidentiality, creating breach reporting procedures, and ensuring proper data management practices. Signing a NDA may provide a legal framework for protection, but without active compliance and enforcement, the agreement itself is merely words on paper.

Conclusion

NDAs are far more than routine documents in government contracting—they are essential tools for protecting sensitive information, ensuring compliance with federal regulations, and fostering trust in business relationships. Misconceptions, such as treating NDAs as "boilerplate," assuming they must always be mutual, or believing they guarantee safety upon signature, can undermine their effectiveness and create unnecessary risk.

By understanding the purpose of NDAs and addressing these misconceptions, contracting professionals can approach NDAs with the care, diligence, and precision they require. This will ensure that NDAs remain a powerful safeguard for protecting proprietary or sensitive information.

Chapter 2
The Basics

Introduction

While NDAs are widely used across all kinds of industries, they hold particular significance for government contractors, where the sharing of technical, financial, and competitive information is often necessary to explore collaboration opportunities.

Think of a NDA as the formal rules of engagement during the "dating period" of a business relationship, where both companies explore potential collaboration but have not yet solidified a formal agreement.

Consider this analogy:

- **"Dating" Stage:** NDA Execution – Sharing proprietary and/or sensitive data for evaluation.

- **"Engagement" Stage:** Teaming Agreement – A structured plan to work together.

- **"Marriage" Stage:** Contract Award – A formal, legally binding relationship.

NDAs vary in length, content, structure, layout, and complexity depending on their purpose, but their core intent remains the same: to safeguard valuable information and establish trust between parties.

Common Names for NDAs

While "Non-Disclosure Agreement" is the most commonly used term in the realm of government contracting, NDAs may go by different names depending on industry, region, or context. Regardless of the title, the purpose remains consistent: protecting shared information.

Alternative Name	Common Usage
Confidential Agreement (CA)	United Kingdom, Australia
Proprietary Information Agreement (PIA)	U.S. Government Contracting
Secrecy Agreement (SA)	Commercial and legal industries
Confidential Disclosure Agreement (CDA)	Research, scientific, and healthcare fields

Key Takeaway: The name doesn't matter—what matters is the content and expected enforceability of the document

Most Common Uses of NDAs

NDAs are widely used across various industries and business functions to safeguard proprietary information. In government contracting, they are particularly important during the pre-proposal phase, especially when contractors explore a teaming approach for proposal submissions. Before entering into a formal teaming agreement, companies often exchange confidential data such as past performance records, pricing strategies, or technical capabilities to assess compatibility and mutual benefits.

Another common scenario involves the use of NDAs when hiring consultants or independent contractors for specialized tasks or short-term engagements. These specialists are frequently brought on during the pre-proposal phase, where they gain access to sensitive information necessary to fulfill specific project requirements.

Types of NDAs

NDAs are classified into three main types, depending on the flow of information:

1. **Unilateral NDAs:**
    - Only one party discloses confidential information.
    - Example: A prime contractor shares sensitive data with a subcontractor for proposal preparation.

2. **Bilateral (Mutual) NDAs:**
    - Both parties exchange and agree to protect each other's confidential information.
    - Example: Two companies sharing past performance data during teaming discussions.

3. **Multilateral (Tripartite) NDAs:**
    - Involve three or more parties exchanging confidential information.
    - Example 1: A Joint Venture (JV) contractor coordinating with multiple subcontractors on a large proposal.
    - Example 2: A team of contractors must gain access to a government network or server that stores a firms protected information in order to complete their contractual obligations.

Key Functions of NDAs

NDAs serve three primary functions:

1. **Protect Confidential Information:** NDAs create a legal obligation for the receiving party to safeguard sensitive information. Breaches can result in damages, injunctive relief, or other remedies.

2. **Preserve Intellectual Property Rights:** Sharing technical designs or inventions without a NDA could jeopardize patent rights. NDAs ensure inventors maintain control over their intellectual property.

3. **Define Boundaries:** NDAs clearly identify what information is confidential and establish exclusions for publicly available or independently developed information.

When are NDAs Required for Government Contractors?

Interestingly, federal acquisition regulations do not require NDAs between government contractors. Companies often demand NDAs as a precaution and this approach is strictly a business decision. Several laws do exist that encourage companies to protect their proprietary and sensitive information, creating a business need for NDAs in the following situations:

- Exploring teaming arrangements for joint proposals.
- Engaging consultants, vendors, or subcontractors who will access sensitive data.
- Sharing intellectual property, technical designs, or financial information.

However, NDAs should not be used automatically. Contractors must evaluate whether the information truly warrants protection before executing an NDA. Overusing NDAs can be time-consuming and costly to administer.

Practical Tip: Avoid overuse. If no proprietary data will be shared, executing a NDA may be unnecessary and create unnecessary administrative burdens.

Structure and Length of NDAs

A typical NDA includes the following components:

Section	Purpose
Introduction and Definitions	Identifies the parties and defines key terms.
Purpose of Disclosure	Specifies why the information is being shared.
Recipient Obligations	Outlines steps to protect shared information.
Exclusions	Defines what is *not* considered confidential.
Term and Duration	Establishes the NDA's validity period.
Remedies for Breach	Describes consequences for unauthorized disclosure.

Most NDAs range from **4–8 pages**, ensuring clarity without unnecessary complexity.

The Importance of Due Diligence

Before entering an NDA, both parties must conduct due diligence to confirm the other party's credibility and assess potential risks. Key goals of due diligence include:

- Confirming the company's financial stability.
- Verifying technical capabilities.
- Reviewing past performance ratings and legal history.
- Identifying reputational risks or conflicts of interest.

Example Due Diligence Checklist:	
Category	**Objective**
Financial Stability	Assess ability to fulfill obligations.
Technical Capabilities	Verify claimed expertise and systems.
Past Performance	Evaluate reliability and delivery record.
Reputation	Identify legal disputes or ethical concerns.

Avoiding Common NDA Pitfalls

To reinforce the importance of due diligence and careful NDA execution, here are two real-world lessons:

- **Example 1:** A contractor failed to verify a subcontractor's reputation before executing an NDA, leading to misuse of shared technical data.
- **Example 2:** A firm disclosed proprietary IP under a vague NDA, resulting in the loss of patent rights when the recipient exploited residual information.

Key Lesson: Conduct due diligence and tailor NDAs to the specific risks and circumstances of the relationship.

When a NDA May Not Be Necessary

Not every business interaction requires an NDA. For example:

- **High-Level Discussions:** Early conversations without the need to share or exchange proprietary data.
- **Publicly Available Information:** No NDA is needed if the data to be shared is not sensitive or proprietary.
- **Market Research:** Generic information sharing that does not involve IP or strategies.

Conclusion

NDAs are foundational tools in government contracting, enabling companies to share sensitive data while protecting their interests. By understanding NDA types, functions, structure, and risks (and conducting thorough due diligence) contractors can use NDAs strategically to build trust and safeguard valuable information. Conducting due diligence and evaluating the true need for a NDA ensures these agreements remain practical, enforceable, and valuable. Remember, a NDA is not just a formality; it's a critical instrument of protection, accountability, and partnership.

Chapter 3
Key Players and Stakeholders

Introduction

In government contracting, successfully drafting, negotiating, and managing Non-Disclosure Agreements (NDAs) requires input from multiple internal and external stakeholders. Unlike simpler commercial contracts, NDAs in federal contracting must meet strict operational, legal, and regulatory requirements. Each stakeholder brings a unique set of skills and responsibilities to ensure that NDAs are fair, enforceable, and aligned with both compliance obligations and project goals.

For new contracting professionals, understanding the roles of these stakeholders and their contributions is critical to navigating the NDA process effectively. This chapter identifies the key players involved and explains how their collaboration ensures the success of the agreement.

Internal Stakeholders

Internal stakeholders are individuals or teams within an organization who contribute directly to NDA development, negotiation, and enforcement. Their expertise ensures the NDA aligns with legal requirements and operational objectives.

Contracting Professionals

Contracting professionals, such as Contract Managers, Administrators, or Specialists, are on the frontlines of the NDA process. They are responsible for preparing, reviewing, and negotiating the proposed agreement to ensure it aligns with the scope of work and supports the organization's business goals. Contracting professionals also negotiate key clauses, such as

Permitted Use and *Return of Information*, to achieve a fair balance of protections and risks.

Their role is critical because they focus on practical implementation, ensuring the NDA avoids overly broad terms while supporting operational needs. For example, they verify that the *Permitted Use* clause restricts the data's application to specific purposes like proposal development or contract performance. Without this attention to detail, NDAs can inadvertently permit improper data usage.

Legal Counsel

Legal counsel, including in-house attorneys or external advisors specializing in government contracting, ensures the NDA is legally sound and enforceable. Their role includes identifying legal risks, addressing ambiguities, and confirming compliance with laws such as FAR, DFARS, or export control regulations like ITAR and EAR.

Legal teams also focus on clauses that influence risk and enforceability, such as *Choice of Law* and *Remedies for Breach*. For instance, if a NDA lacks clarity on protecting trade secrets indefinitely, legal counsel will step in to amend the clause, ensuring long-term enforceability. Their input is vital to preventing litigation risks and regulatory penalties.

Compliance Teams

Compliance teams, including Compliance Officers, Export Control Managers, and Data Privacy Specialists, ensure that NDAs adhere to federal regulations, internal policies, and industry standards. They focus on the proper handling of Controlled Unclassified Information (CUI) and technical data subject to export control laws.

Compliance teams play a key role in identifying conflicts with existing regulatory obligations and monitoring risks that arise when sharing data across borders. For example, if technical data must be shared with a foreign subcontractor, compliance teams will verify ITAR compliance and secure necessary licenses.

Program and Technical Teams

Program managers, engineers, IT specialists, and subject matter experts (SMEs) are the custodians of confidential or proprietary information during a project. Their role involves identifying what data requires protection, communicating why it must be shared, and implementing standards of care for safeguarding that information.

Program and technical teams ensure that the NDA's requirements are operationally feasible. For instance, they may classify specific data, such as proprietary schematics or CUI, that requires specialized handling and long-term confidentiality protections. Their input is essential to defining the scope of the NDA and avoiding unintentional breaches.

External Stakeholders

External stakeholders are individuals or organizations outside of your company who are party to the NDA. They play a significant role in determining the agreement's scope, obligations, and protections.

Subcontractors

Subcontractors often need access to another firms proprietary data to fulfill their roles on a government contract. NDAs clarify what information can be shared, outline restrictions on its use and disclosure, and require subcontractors to extend confidentiality obligations to their personnel or third-party vendors. Clear NDAs enable subcontractors to complete their work while protecting the prime contractor's sensitive information.

Teaming Partners

Teaming Agreements involve collaboration among multiple organizations to pursue a government contract. NDAs in these situations safeguard each party's proprietary data, including pricing strategies and technical information, ensuring it cannot be misused for unauthorized purposes or competing bids. These agreements create trust among teaming partners, facilitating open collaboration.

Vendors and Consultants

Vendors and consultants may require access to confidential information to provide essential services, such as IT support, legal advice, or operational solutions. NDAs ensure these third parties maintain confidentiality and prevent the misuse of shared data. Because vendors and consultants often operate outside the core contract, robust NDAs are critical to maintaining data protection.

Why Stakeholder Coordination is Critical

Effective NDA management requires seamless coordination among all stakeholders.

When the objectives of stakeholders are not aligned, the NDA process can become delayed, ambiguous terms may go unnoticed, and noncompliance risks can emerge. For example, failure to involve compliance teams could result in violations of export control laws, while a lack of input from program teams might lead to unrealistic confidentiality obligations that hinder operations.

Engaging stakeholders early and maintaining open communication throughout the NDA process ensures the agreement is fair, clear, and actionable. Proper coordination minimizes delays, mitigates risks, and promotes stronger partnerships.

Conclusion

NDAs are not created or managed in isolation—they are collaborative agreements that rely on the expertise of both internal and external stakeholders. Contracting professionals ensure the NDA aligns with business needs, legal counsel focuses on enforceability and risk mitigation, and compliance teams uphold regulatory requirements. Program and technical teams, as the custodians of confidential information, ensure that operational realities align with NDA obligations.

For external stakeholders, such as subcontractors, teaming partners, and vendors, NDAs provide the framework to enable collaboration while protecting sensitive data. By understanding each stakeholder's role and ensuring coordinated efforts, contracting professionals can streamline the NDA process, reduce risk, and maintain compliance in the complex world of government contracting.

Part II
Dissecting and Mastering NDA Clauses

Chapter 4
Dissecting and Mastering NDA Clauses

Introduction

Non-Disclosure Agreements (NDAs) may appear simple at first glance—a legal tool to safeguard confidential information—but the real power of a NDA lies in its clauses. Each clause is a precision instrument, carefully drafted to balance protection, clarity, and enforceability. However, understanding these clauses in depth is essential for government contractors, where missteps can lead to unintended disclosures, disputes, or even loss of business opportunities.

In this chapter, we pull back the curtain on the individual building blocks of an NDA. Whether you are a prime contractor, subcontractor, or consultant, mastering the clauses within a NDA ensures you are equipped to protect your sensitive data, fulfill your obligations, and avoid unnecessary risks. This chapter provides a **detailed analysis** of the most commonly used clauses, as well as the ones that are included only under specific circumstances.

The Anatomy of a NDA Clause

In this chapter, you will learn to analyze clauses through the following key lenses:

1. **Purpose and Function:** What does the clause do? Why is it included? For example, a **"Definition of Confidential Information"** clause serves to set clear boundaries on what is protected under the agreement.

2. **Importance and Risks:** Why is the clause important for government contractors? What risks arise if it is poorly written or omitted?

3. **Examples:** To ground the explanation, we provide clear, real-world examples of commonly used language for each clause. This ensures you can **recognize** the clause in your NDAs or use it as a template during negotiations.

4. **Companion Clauses:** Many NDA clauses are interconnected. Removing or modifying one can impact the effectiveness of another. For example, the **"Return or Destruction of Information"** clause often works hand-in-hand with the **"Term and Duration"** clause. Companion clauses highlight these interdependencies to help you identify potential gaps or conflicts in your agreement.

About Companion Clauses:

While many companion clauses are mutual, the relationship is not guaranteed to be reciprocal. When drafting or negotiating NDAs, contractors should carefully analyze how clauses interact (whether mutually or one-directionally), and ensure the overall agreement reflects the intended protections and obligations. The relationship between the clauses depends on their purpose and structure. Some clauses are mutually dependent, meaning each clause supports or governs the other equally. In other situations, the relationship is one-sided, where one clause relies on the other, but the reverse is not true.

Companion clauses are considered mutual when they are interconnected, with both clauses relying on or modifying one another's application. However, it is more common for the relationship between companion clauses to be one-directional, where one clause benefits from or refers to the other without a reciprocal dependency. For example, the relationship between a Survival clause and a Confidentiality clause demonstrates a one-sided connection. The Survival clause extends confidentiality obligations beyond the NDA's termination, ensuring continued protection of sensitive information. While the Confidentiality clause relies on the Survival clause for this extended protection, the Survival clause is not inherently dependent on the Confidentiality clause, as it may also apply to other provisions such as indemnity or governing law.

Recognizing whether companion clauses are mutual or one-sided is crucial during the negotiation process. Ensuring that one-sided relationships are clearly evaluated will avoid gaps or ambiguity in the final agreement. Additionally, a skilled negotiator understands that when one clause relies heavily on another, removing or modifying either clause can inadvertently (perhaps even intentionally) weaken the overall agreement.

Clause Analysis

The variety in format and content for each clause analysis reflects the **nuanced nature** of NDAs. Some clauses require deeper discussion due to their complexity or relevance, while others can be explained succinctly. Our goal is to ensure each clause receives the level of attention it deserves, without forcing a rigid, cookie-cutter format that dilutes its significance.

How to Use This Chapter

This chapter is not designed to be read from start to finish in a single sitting. Instead, consider it a **reference guide** you can return to when:

- You need to draft or review an NDA.
- You encounter an unfamiliar clause and want to understand its purpose.
- You are negotiating a NDA and need examples or talking points.

Each clause section is self-contained, allowing you to focus on the clauses most relevant to your needs.

Conclusion

By the end of this chapter, you will have a deeper understanding of how individual NDA clauses operate, why they matter, and how they interact with one another. You will gain the confidence to draft, review, and negotiate NDAs that truly protect your company's interests without creating unnecessary risks.

Whether you are the disclosing party looking to safeguard sensitive information or the receiving party trying to manage obligations, mastering NDA clauses is a **critical skill** for government contracting professionals.

Let's begin the journey by dissecting these clauses one by one.

LEGAL NAMES OF ALL PARTIES

In government contracting, precision is everything - especially when it comes to legal agreements. One critical detail that can't be overlooked in a Non-Disclosure Agreement (NDA) is the inclusion of the **legal names of all parties involved**. Clearly stating the full legal names ensure there is no ambiguity about who is bound by the agreement. Without this clarity, the NDA could be rendered unenforceable, leaving sensitive information unprotected and exposing contractors to significant legal and financial risks.

Using the correct legal names—such as "XYZ Technologies, Inc." instead of "XYZ Technologies" eliminates confusion about which entity is party to the agreement. Therefore, your due diligence efforts should include processes for the verification of even the most basic data. Verify the information you have been provided with SAMs, the other party's website, and various social media venues.

This is especially important for contractors with subsidiaries or affiliates, as failing to distinguish between entities could lead to loopholes in enforcement. For instance, if a NDA doesn't specify the exact legal name of a subcontractor, that subcontractor could argue that they were not bound by the agreement.

Including full legal names also helps clarify the scope of the agreement and defines who is authorized to share and receive protected information. This clarity is essential in highly regulated environments, where unauthorized disclosures can lead to compliance violations, security breaches, or even contract termination. NDAs should leave no room for interpretation. Government clients expect contractors to demonstrate professionalism and meticulous attention to detail, and using precise legal names is part of that responsibility.

Finally, clear identification of parties fosters accountability and trust. By explicitly naming each party, the NDA establishes a formal relationship and ensures that all parties understand their rights and obligations. This is particularly important where collaboration between primes, subcontractors, and third parties often involves complex legal and operational dynamics.

Including legal names in NDAs is more than a formality—it's a safeguard that ensures enforceability, protects sensitive information, and reinforces the integrity of the contracting process. In a field where precision matters, contractors can't afford to leave this detail to chance.

Companion Clauses

The Legal Names of All Parties Clause must work in harmony with the following Companion Clauses to produce an effective NDA:

Companion Clauses	**Why It's Important**
Definitions	Ensures that the roles of the parties (e.g., "Disclosing Party" and "Receiving Party") are unambiguously stated
Affiliates and Third Parties	Builds on the legal names to clarify whether affiliates, subsidiaries, or related entities of the receiving party are also bound by the NDA
Responsible Parties	Identifies individuals within the named parties who are authorized to disclose or receive information

Companion Clauses	Why It's Important
Assignment	Prevents parties from transferring their obligations under the NDA to third parties without consent.
Change of Control or Ownership	Addresses how a change in ownership or control impacts the agreement's enforceability.

DEFINITIONS

The **Definitions Clause** establishes a shared understanding of the agreement's key terms, ensuring consistent interpretation by both parties. In recent years, many contractors have moved away from including a standalone clause dedicated to definitions, instead embedding key definitions within the preamble or scattered throughout the agreement's broader subject matter sections. While this approach can streamline the document, it places a greater burden on reviewers to carefully analyze the entire NDA to identify and understand the defined terms. This shift underscores the importance of avoiding a "checklist mentality" and instead approaching the NDA with a detailed and critical eye to ensure no terms are overlooked or misinterpreted.

Why the Definitions Clause Matters

The Definitions Clause provides clarity and eliminates confusion by explicitly defining key terms used throughout the NDA. It ensures all parties to the agreement share a common understanding of what certain words or phrases mean. This clarity serves no less than three critical purposes:

1. **Precision and Consistency**
   NDAs often use technical, legal, or industry-specific terms that may carry different meanings depending on the context. The Definitions Clause ensures that these terms are used consistently throughout the agreement. For example, terms like "Confidential Information," "Disclosing Party," or "Receiving Party" are clarified up front, leaving no room for misinterpretation.
2. **Scope of Protection**
   A Definitions Clause plays a central role in defining the scope of the NDA. For instance, the definition of "Confidential Information" determines what data or materials are protected under the agreement. A broad or vague definition could inadvertently exclude critical

information, leaving it unprotected, while an overly broad definition could be deemed unenforceable.

3. **Supporting Enforcement**
   Clarity in definitions strengthens the enforceability of the NDA. Courts are far more likely to uphold agreements that use clear, unambiguous language. A well-drafted Definitions Clause provides a strong foundation for enforcement if a breach occurs.

What Should a Definitions Clause Address?

An effective Definitions Clause should identify and define the key terms that are critical to the NDA's purpose. While each agreement may vary depending on the needs of the parties, the following terms are commonly addressed:

1. **Confidential Information**
   Clearly define what constitutes "Confidential Information," including examples such as technical data, trade secrets, pricing, software, proposals, or business strategies.
   Include exceptions for publicly available information or data independently developed by the receiving party.

2. **Disclosing Party and Receiving Party**
   Identify the parties to the agreement and define their roles. The **Disclosing Party** is the entity sharing the confidential information, while the **Receiving Party** is the entity receiving and protecting it.

3. **Permitted Use**
   Define the specific purpose for which confidential information may be used (e.g., proposal preparation for Solicitation Number [Insert Solicitation Number], or subcontract negotiations for prime contract number [Insert Prime Contract Number].).

4. **Term of Agreement**
   Define how long the obligations of confidentiality remain in effect.

5. **Representatives or Affiliates**
   Clarify whether employees, subcontractors, consultants, or affiliates of the receiving party are also bound by the NDA.

6. **Materials and Media**
   Specify the forms of confidential information, such as oral, written, digital, or physical materials.

What the Clause Should Allow and Prohibit

- **Allow**: The clause should allow for sufficient specificity without overly limiting the scope of protection. It should provide clear definitions while leaving room for the agreement's practical application.

- **Prohibit**: Avoid overly broad or vague definitions that could make the NDA unenforceable. For example, defining "Confidential Information" too broadly to include publicly available or unrelated data may render the agreement invalid in court.

Legal Liabilities and Remedies

If terms like "Confidential Information" or "Permitted Use" are poorly defined, the disclosing party may struggle to prove a breach, reducing their ability to recover damages or seek injunctive relief.

For example:

- A narrowly defined "Confidential Information" clause may inadvertently exclude sensitive data, leaving it unprotected.

- Conversely, a well-defined term strengthens the disclosing party's ability to enforce the agreement, ensuring they can seek legal remedies like monetary damages, injunctive relief, or termination of access to the information.

Example of an Industry Standard Definitions Clause

"For the purposes of this Agreement: (a) 'Confidential Information' means any technical, financial, or business information disclosed by the Disclosing Party to the Receiving Party, whether in written, oral, electronic, or other forms, and marked or otherwise identified as confidential; (b) 'Disclosing Party' means [Full Legal Name of Entity]; (c) 'Receiving Party' means [Full Legal Name of Entity]; and (d) 'Permitted Use' means the use of Confidential Information solely for the purpose of evaluating or performing [specific project or collaboration] and for no other purpose."

By clearly defining key terms, the clause eliminates ambiguity, reduces the risk of disputes, and strengthens enforceability. Contractors who overlook this clause risk misunderstandings, unenforceable agreements, and weakened legal protections. In short, clarity in definitions creates confidence in compliance—a critical outcome for any government contractor

Companion Clauses

The Definitions Clause must work in harmony with the following Companion Clauses to produce an effective NDA:

Companion Clauses	Why It's Important
Covered Information	Clearly defines what constitutes Protected Information.
Exclusions from Protection	Provides exceptions to the definition of confidential information.
Specific Purpose	Specifies for what purposes the Confidential / Proprietary Information can and cannot be used.
Survivability	Extends confidentiality obligations beyond the termination of the agreement.
Notice of Breach	Requires the receiving party to promptly notify the disclosing party if covered information is disclosed or mishandled.

EFFECTIVE DATE

One common yet crucial detail that must not be overlooked in Non-Disclosure Agreements (NDAs) is the effective date. This seemingly simple term plays a foundational role in defining when the agreement's obligations and protections begin. An undefined or ambiguous effective date can lead to legal, financial, and reputational risks, making it essential for successful contract administration.

The effective date establishes a clear starting point for the confidentiality obligations outlined in the NDA. It ensures that any information disclosed after this date is covered by the agreement's protections. For government contractors, where sensitive information such as trade secrets or classified materials is frequently exchanged, this clarity is critical. Without a defined effective date, disputes can arise over whether information disclosed before or after the agreement was signed is protected—creating unnecessary vulnerabilities and potential liabilities.

Beyond providing immediate clarity, the effective date is also crucial for managing the lifecycle of the NDA, particularly termination and survival clauses. Many NDAs specify a "protection period," during which the obligations of confidentiality continue even after the agreement ends. The effective date serves as the anchor for these timelines, ensuring both parties have a shared understanding of their responsibilities. This is especially important for long-term government contracts, where overlapping timelines and shifting priorities can make it easy to lose track of obligations.

As routine practice, the effective date is identified in the preamble of the document. Normally it is identified in the very first sentence and will look something similar to this

> *This Agreement entered into as of* **18 April 202X** *(effective date), by and between* **Mr. Prime**

> ***Contractor Inc***, *organized and existing under the laws of the State of Texas and having its principal offices at 123 Main Street, Dusty City; Texas 98765 (hereinafter called "**Mr. Prime**") and XYZ company, organized and existing under the laws of the State of **VA**, and having its principal office at **1013 Back Street**; **Townville**, **VA 65298** (hereinafter called "**XYZ**")*

For agreements of this nature, the actual date of signature, or date of agreement execution, is merely a matter of record and a clarifying statement of acceptance of the specific terms of the agreement, but protections are only granted to the information that was exchanged on or after the effective date. Information exchanged prior to the effective date is not normally considered information that must be protected.

In some instances, an actual date is not specifically identified, but the effective date is intended to be the date of execution of the NDA. This is a fairly common approach and is typical in situations where the parties have internal review processes with long lead times, and a firm date for signature cannot be predicted with any accuracy. In those situations, the effective date may be identified by a clause written similar to this example:

> *This Agreement shall become effective upon the last date of execution by the Parties and, unless earlier terminated by either party with sixty days prior written notice, shall remain in effect for a period of one (1) year thereafter.*

Another approach some contractors employ is the use of a standalone clause to identify the effective date, like this example:

> *Article III – Effective Date*

This agreement shall become effective upon the earlier occurrence of either: (a) the latest date signed by either of the parties, or (b) 8 October 20XY.

Or

Article III – Effective Date

This agreement shall become effective on 8 October 20XY.

This approach is the most direct and clear. Agreements that contain a clause devoted to the statement of the agreements effective date leave little room for misinterpretation or misunderstandings.

Companion Clauses

The Effective Date Clause must work in harmony with the following Companion Clauses to produce an effective NDA:

Companion Clauses	Why It's Important
Term or Duration Period	Works directly with the Effective Date to define when the NDA starts and how long confidentiality obligations remain in effect.
Survivability	Extends confidentiality obligations beyond the termination of the agreement.
Standards of Care	Establishes the receiving party's duty to protect and safeguard the

Companion Clauses	Why It's Important
	proprietary information as of the Effective Date.
Return of Proprietary Information	Triggered at the end of the NDA's term, which begins on the Effective Date
Termination	Provides an exit mechanism for ending the NDA.

SPECIFIC PURPOSE

The purpose serves as the foundation of the NDA, outlining why proprietary or confidential information is being shared and establishing boundaries for its use. Whether it's collaborating on a proposal for a government solicitation or discussing a classified project, specifying the purpose ensures the agreement stays focused and effective.

When the purpose of a NDA is too vague, it opens the door to potential misuse or misunderstanding of the shared information. For instance, technical data shared for a particular proposal might inadvertently, or intentionally, be repurposed for a completely different project. Defining a focused purpose prevents this by ensuring that sensitive information is used only for its intended context. In government contracting, where intellectual property and national security are often at stake, this clarity isn't just good practice — it's essential.

A well-defined purpose also reduces the likelihood of disputes about the scope of permissible disclosures. Both parties gain a shared understanding of what's covered under the agreement, minimizing the risk of accidental breaches or claims of misuse. Additionally, narrowing the purpose naturally limits the duration and scope of the NDA. This prevents the agreement from becoming unnecessarily broad, which could create compliance headaches or liabilities for contractors.

How the purpose is defined and documented within the NDA can vary. It might appear in the preamble as part of the introductory language, such as:

> "**WHEREAS,** Mr. Prime Contractor Inc. and XYZ company are desirous of exchanging proprietary information relating to "Widget enHancement and Applied Techniques (WHAT)" and hereafter referred to as the "Program" or "Purpose". The

exchange of information considered company sensitive or proprietary is expected to be necessary for the parties to explore the likelihood of potential teaming in response to the Government's solicitation number BSPH602X1234.

Alternatively, it can be written as a standalone clause, for example:

Article 1 – The Purpose

Mr. Prime Contractor Inc. and XYZ company intend to disclose to each other certain Confidential or Proprietary Information as further described in Article 2 of this agreement solely for the purpose of: "Widget enHancement and Applied Techniques (WHAT)", the "Purpose".

Both approaches are effective and acceptable. The ultimate goal is to have a clearly defined purpose that is restricts the use of the information exchanged to only a specific program or effort.

In the examples above each stated that the purpose of the agreement was related to the "Widget enHancement and Applied Techniques (WHAT)" effort. Unfortunately, all too often a contractors marketing team will request a broad, overarching NDA that covers a high level technology, or maybe even a line of businesses. In those situations the purpose often will resemble something of this nature:

Article 1 – The Purpose

Mr. Prime Contractor Inc. and XYZ company intend to disclose to each other certain Confidential Information and/or Proprietary Information for the purpose of identifying future areas of interest in any field or technological area that may benefit from Widget Enhancement and

> *applied Techniques (WHAT) and may therefore result in potential teaming opportunities.*

Non-Disclosure Agreements should only be initiated when a specific need has been identified that has a high probability of a teaming or subcontracting relationship developing. Agreements written for broad purposes may not be enforceable or legally binding agreements. Furthermore, these types of agreements carry high levels of unnecessary RISK that is associated with the potential release of sensitive information into the public domain, and therefore it is not protectable under any other NDA for any other purpose. For these reasons, the inherent risk associated with NDAs that have an undefined or broad purpose far outweighs any potential benefits and therefore, as routine sound business practice, they should always be avoided.

For subcontractors, a purpose clause can also include stronger protection to ensure that information is not misused. For instance:

> *"The purpose of this NDA is to further discussions between the parties regarding the Widget enHancement and Applied Techniques (WHAT) program. If either party does not participate in submitting a proposal, all exchanged information must be returned immediately to the disclosing party and cannot be used for any other purpose."*

This level of specificity ensures clear expectations, protects intellectual property, and reinforces trust between the parties.

NDAs are more than just formalities, they're essential tools for safeguarding information and maintaining compliance. By taking the time to clearly define the purpose, contracting professionals can minimize risks, ensure mutual understanding, and set the stage for successful collaborations.

Companion Clauses

The Specific Purpose Clause must work in harmony with the following Companion Clauses to produce an effective NDA:

Companion Clauses	Why It's Important
Specific Purpose	Specifies for what purposes the Confidential / Proprietary Information can and cannot be used.
Standards of Care	Sets clear obligations for the receiving party to protect the information shared.
Restricted Use	Explicitly states that confidential information cannot be used for any purpose other than what is defined
Information Excluded from Protection	Clarifies what information does *not* fall under the confidentiality obligations of the NDA
Remedies for Breach	Provides recourse if a breach occurs during the term of the NDA.

RECIPENT OBLIGATIONS

From proprietary pricing strategies to technical designs and past performance records, prime contractors and subcontractors must share data to achieve common goals. However, sharing such valuable information comes with risks, which makes The Recipient Obligations Clause one of the most vital components of an NDA. This provision sets clear rules for how the receiving party must handle, protect, and use the disclosing party's proprietary information. When well-drafted, this clause not only protects sensitive data but also fosters trust and reduces potential disputes.

Benefits of the Recipient Obligations Clause

The **Recipient Obligations** clause is critical because it:

1. **Defines Clear Responsibilities:**
   By outlining specific obligations, the clause removes ambiguity and ensures the receiving party understands what is expected. This clarity reduces the likelihood of accidental breaches or disputes over misinterpretations.

2. **Protects Proprietary Information:**
   The clause mandates how information is handled, shared, and used, ensuring the disclosing party's proprietary data is not misused or leaked to unauthorized parties.

3. **Encourages Trust and Collaboration:**
   When both parties feel secure that their information is protected, they are more likely to share meaningful insights, fostering stronger partnerships and better collaboration on projects.

4. **Reduces Risk of Litigation:**
   A well-crafted Recipient Obligations clause establishes enforceable terms, reducing the likelihood of disputes escalating into costly legal battles.

Why Are Recipient Obligations Important?

Both the disclosing and receiving parties have a vested interest in clearly defining the recipient's obligations for protecting proprietary information. For the Disclosing Party, the provision ensures their sensitive data is protected from misuse or disclosure, and it established the groundwork for enforcement if a breach occurs. For the Receiving Party, the provision clarifies their responsibilities, which reduces the risk of unintentional violations.

What Should the Clause Address, Allow, and Prohibit?

To maximize its effectiveness, a Recipient Obligations clause should:

1. **Require Markings** - The clause should require that the specific information to be protected is required to be labeled as "confidential" or "proprietary."

2. **Limit the Purpose of Use-** The recipient must use the information solely for the purposes outlined in the NDA (e.g., proposal development, evaluation, or project execution).

3. **Restrict Access to a Need-to-Know Basis** - Limiting access to authorized personnel ensures the information is not unnecessarily exposed within the recipient's organization.

4. **Prohibit Unauthorized Copies or Distribution** - The clause should restrict the recipient from making copies or excerpts of the information without explicit written consent.

5. **Allow FAR-Compliant Disclosures to the U.S. Government** - To align with government contracting and proposal preparation and submittal practices, the clause should permit

disclosure to federal customers under strict confidentiality guidelines.

Below is an example of a Recipient Obligations clause:

Recipient Obligations

With respect to proprietary information so identified, both parties agree to the following:

(a) The recipient shall hold it in confidence from the date of receipt through the protection period

(b) The recipient shall use it only for information and evaluation purposes in connection with the specific program identified earlier in this document.

(c) The recipient shall make it available only to its employees having a "need to know" in order to carry out their respective functions in connection with the receiving party's effort on the Program.

(d) The recipient will NOT make any copy or excerpt of Proprietary Information without the disclosing party's prior written consent.

(e) The recipient shall not otherwise use or disclose any protected information to third parties without written authorization of the disclosing party. If the purpose of this agreement it to eventually submit a proposal to any branch or division of the US Government, the receiving party may disclose protected information to the US

> *Government customer on a confidential basis provided the information bears the restrictive legend required by Federal Acquisition Regulation (FAR).*
>
> *(f) Each party shall bear all costs and expenses incurred by it under or in connection with this Agreement. This Agreement is intended to provide only for the handling and protection of Proprietary Information. It shall not be construed as a Teaming, Joint Venture, Partnership, or other similar arrangement. Specifically, this Agreement shall not be construed in any manner to be an obligation to enter into a formal Teaming Agreement, contract or subcontract, nor shall it result in any claim for reimbursement of costs.*

Companion Clauses

The Recipient Obligations Clause must work in concert with other NDA provisions to provide comprehensive protection. Key companion clauses include:

Companion Clauses	**Why It's Important**
Definitions	Clearly defines what constitutes "Confidential or Proprietary Information" and ensure exclusions are appropriately identified
Specific Purpose	Specifies for what purposes the Confidential / Proprietary

Companion Clauses	Why It's Important
	Information can and cannot be used.
Covered Information	Clearly defines what constitutes Protected Information.
Standards of Care	Sets clear obligations for the receiving party to protect the information shared.
Permitted Disclosure	Allows disclosures under defined circumstances.
Restricted Use	Ensures that only confidential, protected data is subject to use limitations.
Information Excluded from Protection	Clarifies what information does *not* fall under the confidentiality obligations of the NDA
Return of Proprietary Information	Requires the receiving party to dispose of confidential information securely, aligning with the Standards of Care for data protection

COVERED INFORMATION

At the heart of every NDA lies the "Covered Information" Clause, which defines the specific types of information that are subject to confidentiality obligations. This clause ensures clarity, minimizes disputes, and provides both parties with a shared understanding of what is—and what isn't—protected.

Why a Covered Information Clause is Essential

Any information that flows between the parties can be considered "Proprietary Information", "Company Sensitive Information" or "Confidential Information", all of which are considered "Covered Information". Therefore, a well-defined Covered Information Clause offers several benefits for parties to an NDA:

1. **Clarity and Precision**
   By explicitly defining the types of information protected, the clause eliminates ambiguity and ensures both parties understand their confidentiality obligations.

2. **Comprehensive Protection**
   Including specific examples of covered information—such as financial data, engineering drawings, trade secrets, and customer identities—ensures that sensitive and proprietary materials are not inadvertently excluded from the agreement's scope.

3. **Prevention of Disputes**
   Ambiguity in what constitutes "covered information" can lead to conflicts or disputes, particularly if one party claims that certain data was not adequately protected. A clear clause avoids such misunderstandings.

4. **Tailored Coverage**

Every business relationship is unique, and the clause allows parties to tailor the NDA to their specific needs, addressing the types of information most relevant to the transaction.

What Should a Covered Information Clause Address?

An effective Covered Information Clause should address the Types of Information granted protections, the format required, necessary marking requirements, and the future or on-going obligations of the parties.

Types of Information: When defining proprietary or confidential information, it's crucial to include everything that might be disclosed during a business transaction. This can be anything the disclosing party deems company sensitive, confidential, or proprietary. The definition should be clear, leaving no room for confusion or ambiguity. Examples may include:

Technical Data	Technical Know-how	Software Programs
Processes	Analytical Methodologies	Budgetary Information
Prototypes	Engineering Drawings	Test Procedures
Test Results	Special Tools	Systems
Pricing Information	Labor Pool Data	Specifications
Financial Data	Business Strategy Info	Special Capabilities

To qualify as covered information, the information should be information that originated with the disclosing party and has not been previously published or otherwise disclosed to the general public. To qualify as Covered information the disclosers information must also be of a nature that has not previously been available without restriction to any party whatsoever, nor normally furnished to others without compensation.

Format of Information: State whether the protection applies to oral, visual, written, demonstrations, and electronic disclosures. When it comes to electronic disclosures, such as emails, anyone involved in sharing or receiving protected information should understand that if they are sending protected information, it should be marked as protected under the non-disclosure agreement. This includes emails, which are a common format for sharing confidential information.

Oral, visual and demonstrative disclosures are always more challenging to address. For oral, visual, and demonstrative disclosures, it is imperative to include a requirement for the disclosing party to reduce the protected information that has been disclosed into a written format that summarizes the disclosure. This written summary should be submitted to the Receiving Party within a specified time (e.g., 10 business days) after the disclosure. The written summary must be marked accordingly and submitted to representatives of the Receiving Party. This is because oral, visual and demonstrative disclosures can lead to conflicts or disputes later, as it may be difficult to recall exactly what information was disclosed and to defend the methods the receiving party exercised in order to protect the disclosure.

Marking Requirements: To ensure that confidential or proprietary written information receives the full protections outlined in a NDA, it's crucial that such information be clearly and properly marked. Ideally, the agreement will require that each page of every document containing proprietary information should bear the necessary markings. This way, if pages are accidentally separated, both parties will still have a clear understanding of their obligation to protect those individual pages as part of the larger, confidential document.

Ongoing Obligations: Address how the confidentiality obligations will apply to future communications, including routine emails, briefings, meetings, or collaborative discussions.

The clause addressing Covered Information sometimes outlines the types of information that don't qualify as confidential or proprietary or specifies information that's intentionally excluded from protection. However, it's more common for this detail to be covered in a separate provision. For the purposes of this discussion, the author has chosen to address Excluded Information in a dedicated clause, which we'll explore later in this chapter.

Risks of Poorly Defined Covered Information

The consequences can be severe, for both parties, when agreements are based on murky or incomplete definitions of the types of information that are granted protection under the agreement.

Imagine two business partners locked in a bitter dispute, each with a different understanding of what the NDA meant to protect. Without explicit definitions, the very purpose of the agreement crumbles, leaving the parties mired in costly litigation.

Or picture a company that inadvertently leaves its crown jewels exposed. Perhaps a vital algorithm or a groundbreaking research finding was not explicitly listed or properly marked as confidential. In the eyes of the law, such oversights can render the information virtually unprotected, like leaving a priceless treasure chest unlocked and unguarded.

The risks extend even further into the courtroom. If a dispute over confidential information ever reaches the courts, a judge may view a vaguely worded NDA as so flawed that it is unenforceable. This means that even if a party has clearly breached their confidentiality obligations, the victimized company may find it impossible to seek legal remedy.

But a poorly defined or incomplete NDA is little more than a flimsy barrier, offering a false sense of security while leaving the very heart of a company's competitive advantage dangerously exposed. The potential risks – from costly disputes and unintended exposure to legal impotence in the face of theft – are simply too great to ignore.

Best Practices for Drafting a Covered Information Clause

1. **Be Specific:** Include detailed examples of covered information, tailored to the nature of the business relationship or project.

2. **Account for All Formats:** Ensure the clause addresses written, electronic, demonstrative, visual, and oral disclosures, with specific instructions for each.

3. **Use Marking Standards:** Require written disclosures to be labeled as confidential or proprietary and include guidelines for documenting oral or visual disclosures after meetings, demonstrations, or calls.

4. **Educate Team Members:** Train employees involved in sharing or receiving sensitive information to properly mark and handle materials under the NDA.

For your reference, here's a sample Covered Information Clause

> *"Confidential Information" also referred to as Proprietary Information" shall include, but not be limited to, performance, sales, financial,*

contractual and special marketing information, ideas, software, product capabilities, workflow, technical data and concepts originated by the disclosing party, not previously published or otherwise disclosed to the general public, not previously available without restriction to the receiving party or others, nor normally furnished to others without compensation, and which the disclosing party desires to protect against unrestricted disclosure or competitive use, and which is furnished pursuant to this Non disclosure Agreement and appropriately identified as being proprietary when furnished. "Proprietary Information" includes both (a) technical information and data and (b) business and financial information.

Companion Clauses

The Covered Information Clause must work in harmony with the following Companion Clauses to produce an effective NDA:

Companion Clauses	Why It's Important
Information Excluded from Protection	Clarifies what information does *not* fall under the confidentiality obligations of the NDA
Specific Purpose	Specifies for what purposes the Confidential / Proprietary Information can and cannot be used.
Notice of Breach	Requires the receiving party to promptly notify the disclosing

Companion Clauses	Why It's Important
	party if covered information is disclosed or mishandled.
Survivability	Extends confidentiality obligations beyond the termination of the agreement.
Indemnification	Holds the receiving party accountable for damages caused by the misuse or unauthorized disclosure.

INFORMATION EXCLUDED FROM PROTECTION

For many contracting professionals, the focus is often on what information a NDA protects, when in reality, equally important is to know what information is explicitly not protected by the terms of a NDA . Including an Excluded Information Clause is essential to clearly define what types of information fall outside the scope of confidentiality obligations, providing clarity, mitigating risks, and preventing potential disputes.

Key Types of Excluded Information

The Excluded Information Clause typically addresses the following categories:

1. **Publicly Available Information**
   Information that is already in the public domain or becomes publicly available through no fault of the receiving party, and information that was previously disclosed by the disclosing party to a third party without restriction.

2. **Independently Developed Information**
   Data or insights developed independently by the receiving party without using the disclosing party's confidential information.

3. **Information Legally Obtained from a Third Party**
   Information that the receiving party acquires from another source without breach of confidentiality obligations.

4. **Mutually Agreed Non-Confidential Information**
   Information explicitly agreed upon by both parties as non-confidential.

5. **Required Disclosures**
   Information disclosed pursuant to a court order or other legal requirements.

6. **Pre-Existing Information:**
   Data already in possession of the receiving party before the NDA was signed, provided it was not subject to existing confidentiality obligations.

So why should contractors care about clearly defining what is not covered by an NDA?

The answer lies in the potential risks of ambiguity.

Without explicit exclusions, parties may inadvertently find themselves in breach of the agreement. For instance, if publicly available information or data independently developed by the recipient is not clearly deemed non-confidential, it could lead to unintended confidentiality obligations. This not only creates unnecessary restrictions but could also expose the party to claims of breach should such information be shared or used in a manner the other party deems improper.

Moreover, overly broad NDAs can chill collaboration and innovation. If contractors fear that any information shared, no matter how innocuous or publicly available, could become entangled in restrictive confidentiality obligations, they may be less likely to engage in open and fruitful exchanges. By clearly delineating what is not considered confidential, contractors can foster trust and facilitate the free flow of information necessary for successful partnerships.

What Should an Excluded Information Clause Address?

An effective Excluded Information Clause should:

1. **Clearly Define Exclusions**
   Explicitly list all categories of information that fall outside the scope of confidentiality, ensuring there is no ambiguity.

2. **Allow for Required Disclosures**
   Include provisions that allow disclosure of information when required by law, such as in response to a court order or government mandate.

3. **Prohibit Misuse**
   Ensure that excluded information is not used to circumvent the intent of the NDA. For example, proprietary information should not be labeled as excluded to avoid legitimate confidentiality obligations.

To illustrate, consider the following industry-standard clause

Information Excluded from Protection

Each party covenants and agrees that it will keep in confidence, and prevent the disclosure to any third party, or any person or persons outside its organization or to any unauthorized person, any and all information which is received from the other party under this Non-Disclosure Agreement and has been protected in accordance with requirements of this agreement. Information shall not be afforded the protection of this Agreement from and after the first to occur of the following:

a) *was publicly available (in the public domain) at the time of disclosure, or*

b) *when it is developed by the receiving party independently of the disclosing party, or*

> c) *when it is rightly obtained without restriction to the receiving party from a third party, or*
>
> d) *when it becomes publicly available other than through the fault or negligence of the receiving party, or*
>
> e) *when it is released without restriction by the disclosing party to anyone, including the United States Government, or*
>
> f) *when it is disclosed with the written approval of the other party, or*
>
> g) *when it is disclosed pursuant to the provisions of a court order, or*
>
> h) *The expiration of the mutually agreed period of protection.*
>
> *The provisions of this Paragraph shall supersede the provisions of any inconsistent legend that may be affixed to said information by the disclosing party and the inconsistent provisions of any such legend shall be without any force or effect.*

By defining the boundaries of what is protected and what is not, this clause strengthens the NDA's effectiveness and fosters trust between parties.

Companion Clauses

The Information Excluded from Protection Clause must work in harmony with the following Companion Clauses to produce an effective NDA:

Companion Clauses	Why It's Important
Definitions	Clearly defines what constitutes "Confidential or Proprietary Information" and ensure exclusions are appropriately identified
Covered Information	Clearly defines what constitutes Protected Information.
Restricted Use	Ensures that only confidential, protected data is subject to use limitations.

STANDARDS OF CARE

In the world of federal contracting, sharing sensitive information like trade secrets or proprietary information with other contractors is often a necessary step in collaboration. However, this practice carries inherent risks, especially when working with potential future competitors. For these reasons, the ultimate goal of a Standard of Care clause must be to mitigate or manage the unavoidable inherent risk.

A well-crafted Standard of Care clause in a Non-Disclosure Agreement (NDA) is a critical tool to mitigate these risks. The objective is to establish clear, enforceable terms that define how information will be protected throughout the agreement's duration.

Also referred to as a "Standards for Protection" clause, this provision outlines the diligence required by the receiving party in safeguarding shared information, setting clear expectations, and minimizing the risk of disputes. Below is a example of a clause often seen in federal contracting NDAs:

Standards of Protections

The Receiving Party shall exercise the same degree of care to guard against disclosure or use of Proprietary Information, except as provided herein, as Receiving Party employs with respect to its own Proprietary Information of like importance, but in no event less than reasonable care.

It is important to recognize that the type of proprietary information being disclosed significantly influences what constitutes reasonable care. For example: Highly sensitive technical data may require encryption, secure storage, and restricted access, while general business information might only require access controls and confidentiality agreements with employees.

In order to strike a balance between practicality and enforceability of the agreement, the language you negotiate in any Standard of Care clause should provide both clear definitions and Realistic Standards

Clear Definitions: Define "Proprietary and Confidential Information" precisely to avoid ambiguity. For example, include phrases like "information labeled or otherwise designated as proprietary"

Provide for Realistic Standards: Opt for "commercially reasonable standard of care" language to provide flexibility. If possible, avoid higher standards, such as "absolute protection," which are unrealistic and often unenforceable.

Conversely, the final negotiated clause contained in the agreement should avoid vague obligations and unreasonable standards.

Overly Vague Obligations: Avoid vague terms like "all necessary measures" or "absolute security." Such language creates unrealistic obligations that may be impossible to meet, exposing the receiving party to undue liability.

Unreasonable Standards: Do not commit to a standard higher than what is practical for the nature of the information. For instance, agreeing to treat routine business data with the same rigor as classified government information can lead to operational inefficiencies and unnecessary costs. Care should also be taken to resist clauses that impose disproportionate responsibilities on one party while offering little in return. An unbalanced agreement can harm the long-term relationship between parties.

What is Reasonable?

The governing court's jurisdiction will take into account the sensitivity and value of the information when assessing reasonableness. It is also valid to note that industry standards also serve a role in the determination of the "reasonableness" threshold. For example, in federal contracting, for instance, compliance with standards like NIST 800-171 (for cybersecurity) or other government-mandated safeguards may serve as evidence of reasonable care.

Reasonableness also considers the balance between the cost of protective measures and the risks involved. Courts generally do not expect disproportionate efforts or expenses unless explicitly agreed upon. As in all other matters of contract law, legal precedents are the most obvious predicator of any definition or standard. In the case of Standards of Care, the judicial interpretations of similar clauses in comparable cases provide guidance on what constitutes reasonable effort or behaviors under the circumstances.

A Practical Starting Point

The most effective Standard of Care clause strikes a balance between safeguarding proprietary information and fostering collaboration. It should impose responsibilities proportionate to the sensitivity of the information and be equitable for both parties. Below is a sample clause that aligns with these goals:

> ### *Required Standard of Care*
>
> *The standard of care for protecting Proprietary Information imposed on the party receiving such information will be that degree of care (the same steps, methods and precautions) the receiving party uses to prevent disclosure, acquisition, or use of its*

own Proprietary Information, but no less than a commercially reasonable standard of care.

Each party agrees that it shall protect the confidentiality of and take all reasonable steps and precautions to prevent unauthorized disclosure, acquisition, or use of the Proprietary Information to prevent it from falling into the public domain or the public literature, or to prevent it from falling into the possession of unauthorized persons or entities. Neither party shall be liable for the inadvertent or accidental disclosure of Proprietary Information if such disclosure occurs despite the exercise of the same degree of care as such party normally takes to preserve its own such sensitive information or data, but no less than reasonable care

If either party loses or makes unauthorized disclosure of the other party's protected information, it shall notify such other party immediately, and in writing, of any misappropriation or misuse, by any person or entity, of Proprietary Information that comes to its attention or that it reasonably believes may have occurred at any time during the term of this Agreement.

The party at fault shall take all steps reasonable and necessary to retrieve the lost or improperly disclosed information. Each party shall assume all legal liability for any breach of this Agreement by any of its 3rd party affiliates including any agents, consultants, representatives, subcontractors, vendors, and/or suppliers.

By carefully defining expectations and avoiding unrealistic obligations, contractors can protect sensitive information while building the trust and collaboration necessary for success in the highly competitive federal contracting arena. A well-negotiated Standard of Care clause isn't just a safeguard — It's a strategic advantage.

Companion Clauses

The Standards of Care Clause must work in harmony with the following Companion Clauses to produce an effective NDA:

Companion Clauses	Why It's Important
Definitions	Clearly defines what constitutes "Confidential or Proprietary Information" so the Standards of Care apply only to properly defined protected information.
Specific Purpose	Specifies for what purposes the Confidential / Proprietary Information can and cannot be used.
Notice of Breach	Requires the receiving party to promptly notify the disclosing party if covered information is disclosed or mishandled.
Permitted Disclosure	Allows disclosures under defined circumstances.
Return of Proprietary Information	Requires the receiving party to dispose of confidential information securely, aligning with the Standards of Care for data protection

Companion Clauses	Why It's Important
Information Excluded from Protection	The Standards of Care do not apply to publicly available, previously known, or independently developed information.
Remedies for Breach	Provides recourse if a breach occurs during the term of the NDA.
Liquidated Damages	Predefines the financial consequences of failing to protect the disclosing party's confidential information
Affiliates and Third Parties	Ensures that any third parties or affiliates granted access to the confidential information are also required to adhere to the Standards of Care
Survivability	Extends confidentiality obligations beyond the termination of the agreement.

PERMITTED DISCLOSURE

The **Permitted Disclosures Clause** defines specific scenarios where the receiving party is allowed to share confidential information without breaching the NDA. These scenarios typically include legal requirements, regulatory compliance, disclosures to authorized parties, or use in furtherance of contract performance.

The Value of a Permitted Disclosures Clause

Federal contractors operate in an environment, where the need to share confidential information may arise for legal, regulatory, or operational purposes. A Permitted Disclosures Clause ensures that such disclosures are clearly defined, permissible under the NDA, and do not result in an unintended breach of confidentiality. Key reasons why this clause is essential for contractors include:

Compliance with Legal and Regulatory Requirements: Federal contractors are subject to strict legal and regulatory obligations that may require the disclosure of confidential information. For instance, situations can arise where information must be shared to comply with court orders, subpoenas, government audits, or investigations. A Permitted Disclosures Clause explicitly allows these types of legally required disclosures, ensuring compliance without violating the terms of the NDA.

Operational Flexibility: Successful contract performance often requires collaboration with subcontractors, consultants, or legal advisors. The Permitted Disclosures Clause may allow contractors to share confidential information with these authorized parties on a *need-to-know basis*. By enabling disclosures for operational purposes, the clause ensures that necessary information can be shared without breaching confidentiality obligations.

Avoiding Unintentional Breach: Without a Permitted Disclosures Clause, contractors may unknowingly breach the NDA when disclosing information to meet legal or operational requirements. This creates unnecessary risk and potential liability. By explicitly defining exceptions to confidentiality, the clause minimizes these risks and provides legal protection for disclosures made in good faith and within the agreed parameters.

Clarity and Risk Management: Ambiguity in a NDA can lead to disputes, especially regarding what constitutes a permissible disclosure. A well-crafted Permitted Disclosures Clause brings clarity to the agreement, outlining specific conditions under which disclosures are allowed. This clarity reduces the risk of disagreements, protects both parties from claims of misuse, and promotes confidence in the handling of sensitive information.

By addressing compliance, operational needs, and legal risks, a Permitted Disclosures Clause provides contractors with a vital safeguard. It strikes the necessary balance between confidentiality and practical requirements, ensuring that contractors can meet their obligations without fear of violating the NDA.

What Should a Permitted Disclosures Clause Address?

A well-drafted Permitted Disclosures Clause should:

1. **Define Exceptions to Confidentiality**
   Clearly state the situations where disclosure is allowed, such as:

   - Compliance with laws, regulations, subpoenas, or court orders.

   - Disclosures to employees, subcontractors, or advisors who require the information to fulfill contract-related responsibilities.

- Regulatory submissions, including government audits or performance reviews.

2. **Establish Conditions for Permitted Disclosures**
   - Require the receiving party to limit disclosures to the minimum necessary.
   - Mandate that third parties receiving the information agree to written confidentiality obligations.

3. **Notification Requirements**
   - If disclosure is legally required (e.g., subpoena or court order), require prompt notice to the disclosing party. This allows them to take steps to protect the information (e.g., seeking a protective order).

4. **Prohibit Unauthorized Disclosure Beyond Exceptions**
   - Ensure that disclosures are limited to specified conditions and explicitly prohibit sharing information for unauthorized purposes.

Legal Liabilities and Remedies

Failing to include a Permitted Disclosures Clause creates legal and operational risks for contractors:

- **Unintentional Breach**: Disclosing information to comply with a court order or subcontracting need may inadvertently violate the NDA.

- **Disputes Over Compliance**: Without clearly defined exceptions, disputes can arise over whether disclosures were permissible.

- **Liability**: If the clause is absent or poorly written, contractors may face liability for legal or regulatory disclosures made in good faith.

Remedies:

An effective clause mitigates liability by establishing that authorized disclosures are not a breach. However, unauthorized disclosures outside the scope of the clause could result in:

- Injunctive relief to prevent further unauthorized disclosures.
- Financial damages for harm caused by misuse or improper sharing of confidential information.

Example of an Industry Standard Permitted Disclosures Clause

> *"The Receiving Party may disclose Confidential Information under the following circumstances: (a) when required by applicable law, regulation, or court order, provided the Receiving Party gives prompt written notice to the Disclosing Party (unless prohibited by law) to allow for a protective order or other appropriate remedy; (b) to employees who require access to the Confidential Information for the purposes of performing obligations under this Agreement, provided such individuals are bound by written confidentiality obligations no less restrictive than those set forth herein; or (c) as necessary to comply with government audits, investigations, or regulatory submissions. The Receiving Party shall ensure that any permitted disclosures are limited to the minimum information necessary.*
>
> *Neither party shall be liable for damages resulting from any disclosures of information pursuant to judicial action or Government regulations or for inadvertent disclosure thereof where the customary degree of care has been exercised, provided that upon discovery of such inadvertent disclosure it shall*

have endeavored to correct the effects thereof and to prevent any further inadvertent disclosure"

The **Permitted Disclosures Clause** strikes a balance between confidentiality and the practical realities of operating in a regulated, high-stakes environment. By defining when and how confidential information can be disclosed - whether to comply with legal requirements, facilitate contract performance, or engage authorized third parties - it ensures contractors can meet their obligations without fear of unintentional breach.

Companion Clauses

The Permitted Disclosures Clause must work in harmony with the following Companion Clauses to produce an effective NDA:

Companion Clauses	**Why It's Important**
Specific Purpose	Specifies for what purposes the Confidential / Proprietary Information can and cannot be used.
Standards of Care	Sets clear obligations for the receiving party to protect the information shared.
Notice of Breach	Requires the receiving party to promptly notify the disclosing party if covered information is disclosed or mishandled.
Return of Proprietary Information	Requires the receiving party to dispose of confidential information securely, aligning

Companion Clauses	Why It's Important
	with the Standards of Care for data protection
Survivability	Extends confidentiality obligations beyond the termination of the agreement.

NOTICE OF BREACH

The "Notice of Breach" Clause ensures timely communication and appropriate action if a breach of the NDA occurs, mitigating damages and providing a structured path for resolution.

Why Include a Notice of Breach Clause?

A **Notice of Breach Clause** offers significant benefits that ensure timely action, accountability, and legal protection while fostering trust between contractors.

Early Detection and Mitigation: The most critical benefit of a Notice of Breach Clause is that it ensures the disclosing party is promptly informed of any breach or suspected breach. Early detection allows the disclosing party to take immediate action to contain the damage, whether through securing systems, preventing further unauthorized use, or implementing corrective measures, such as legal action or additional security protocols. Timely notification can often mean the difference between a manageable issue and catastrophic consequences, particularly when sensitive government data or Controlled Unclassified Information (CUI) is involved.

Establishing Accountability: This clause creates a clear obligation for the receiving party to monitor their compliance with the NDA and report breaches as soon as they occur. By requiring transparency and proactive reporting, the Notice of Breach Clause ensures accountability. It holds the receiving party responsible for their handling of confidential information and reinforces the seriousness of their obligations under the agreement.

Legal Protection and Remedies: A Notice of Breach Clause strengthens the disclosing party's ability to pursue legal remedies if a breach occurs. By documenting when the breach was discovered, how it was reported, and what actions followed, this clause creates a clear timeline of events. This record is critical for proving damages in court and demonstrating the disclosing party's diligence in addressing the breach. Without timely notification, the disclosing party may suffer greater harm and face significant challenges when seeking legal redress.

Preservation of Trust

A Notice of Breach Clause provides a critical safety net, ensuring breaches are detected, addressed, and mitigated efficiently while holding the responsible party accountable. This, in turn, protects the integrity of confidential information and strengthens the foundation of trust between contracting partners.

What Should a Notice of Breach Clause Address?

An effective Notice of Breach clause must be clear, enforceable, and practical. Key elements include:

1. **Notification Timeline**
   - Define the timeframe within which the receiving party must notify the disclosing party after discovering a breach or suspected breach (e.g., "within 3 business days").
   - Ensure the timeframe is reasonable to allow for investigation while prioritizing prompt notification.

2. **Method of Notification**
   - Specify the acceptable methods for providing notice, such as written notification via email, certified mail, or another formal communication channel.
   - Include the designated point of contact or addresses for delivering breach notices.

3. **Information to Be Included**
   - Require that the notice includes essential details about the breach:
     - A description of the breach or suspected breach.
     - The date and time the breach was discovered.
     - Steps taken to mitigate the breach.
     - Any known impact or parties affected.

4. **Remedies and Follow-Up Actions**
   - Outline any immediate steps the receiving party must take after a breach, such as containing the breach, cooperating with investigations, and implementing corrective measures.

5. **Prohibitions**
   - Prohibit any delay in notification to avoid compounding the harm. Failure to notify within the specified timeframe may constitute a second independent breach of the NDA.

Legal Liabilities and Remedies

A well-drafted **Notice of Breach clause** establishes enforceable obligations for the receiving party, ensuring accountability if a breach or suspected breach occurs. If the receiving party fails to notify the disclosing party promptly, they may face significant consequences.

First, there is liability. The receiving party can be held responsible for damages caused by their failure to report the breach in a timely manner. This liability is in addition to any harm caused by the breach itself, such as unauthorized disclosure or misuse of confidential information.

Second, legal remedies are available to the disclosing party. These remedies include seeking injunctive relief to prevent further unauthorized use or dissemination of proprietary or confidential information. The disclosing party may also pursue monetary damages to recover financial losses caused by the breach. Additionally, the disclosing party may seek indemnification for costs incurred while addressing the breach, such as legal fees, investigative expenses, and mitigation efforts.

By including a Notice of Breach clause, the agreement provides a clear path for recourse, ensuring that breaches are addressed quickly and the responsible party is held accountable.

Example of an Industry Standard Notice of Breach Clause

> *"The Receiving Party shall promptly notify the Disclosing Party in writing of any unauthorized disclosure, loss, or suspected breach of Confidential Information, no later than five (5) business days from the date the breach is discovered. Such notice shall include a description of the breach, the date it occurred, the actions taken to contain or mitigate the breach, and any additional details reasonably requested by the Disclosing Party. The Receiving Party shall cooperate fully with the Disclosing Party to investigate the breach, mitigate any harm, and prevent further unauthorized disclosures. Failure to provide timely notice shall be deemed a material breach of this Agreement, entitling the Disclosing Party to all available legal and equitable remedies."*

By requiring prompt notification of breaches, this clause enables early detection, mitigation, and accountability, reducing potential harm to the disclosing party.

Companion Clauses

The Notice of Breach Clause must work in harmony with the following Companion Clauses to produce an effective NDA:

Companion Clauses	Why It's Important
Standards of Care	Sets clear obligations for the receiving party to protect the information shared.
Choice of Law	Specifies the legal framework and venue for resolving disputes.
Return of Proprietary Information	Requires the receiving party to dispose of confidential information securely, aligning with the Standards of Care for data protection
Remedies for Breach	Provides recourse if a breach occurs during the term of the NDA.
Alternative Dispute Resolutions	Outlines the mechanism by which disagreements between parties will be addressed.
Liquidated Damages	Predefines the financial consequences of failing to protect the disclosing party's confidential information
Survivability	Extends confidentiality obligations beyond the termination of the agreement.

CHOICE OF LAW

Non-Disclosure Agreements (NDAs) in the federal contracting world occupy a unique position. Unlike procurement contracts governed by the Federal Acquisition Regulation (FAR), NDAs are private agreements between two companies or firms and fall outside the scope of federal oversight. Instead, these legally binding documents are governed by state law, meaning their enforceability depends on the specific legal framework of the state chosen by the parties.

Federal contractors should also be aware that the federal government does not involve itself in the enforcement — or prohibition of enforcement — of NDA terms. Once both parties have signed, the government assumes no responsibility for interpreting or enforcing the agreement, leaving resolution solely in the hands of the courts and the legal system of the relevant state.

Because of this, it's critical for contractors to carefully negotiate and specify the legal jurisdiction that governs the NDA. The choice of jurisdiction can significantly impact the protections, remedies, and overall enforceability of the agreement. Selecting a state with favorable laws for your specific needs can provide a distinct advantage and reduce the risk of unforeseen legal challenges.

For federal contractors navigating these agreements, understanding the interplay between state law and the broader federal contracting environment is essential for protecting sensitive information and maintaining a fair, and enforceable NDA.

Choice of Law Clauses: More Than Just Boilerplate

Choice of law clauses are often dismissed as standard "boilerplate" language, with many businesses failing to recognize their strategic importance. Unfortunately, this oversight can lead to significant unintended consequences.

A poorly considered choice of law clause can result in the application of laws that are unfavorable to your firms' interests, particularly in states with legal frameworks less aligned with federal contracting practices. Additionally, it can drive up litigation costs if disputes arise in jurisdictions with complex or unfamiliar legal systems. Worse, it may introduce uncertainty about the enforceability of the agreement, undermining the very purpose of the agreement.

The purpose of governing law clauses is to provide the parties with clarity about the legal framework that will apply in the event of a dispute. These clauses eliminate ambiguity by explicitly stating which state's laws will govern the interpretation and enforcement of the agreement. This certainty is particularly crucial in federal contracting, where parties often operate across state lines or international borders.

When one party resides in a different jurisdiction, the governing law clause ensures that both parties agree, in advance, on the legal codes and standards that will apply to their relationship. Without this provision, disputes could lead to confusion, delays, or costly litigation over which jurisdiction's laws should prevail. For federal government contract administrators, a well-crafted governing law clause is not just a legal safeguard, it's a strategic tool for minimizing risk and maintaining the integrity of the contractual relationship.

For example, here is a typical Choice of Law Clause that is commonly found in NDAs:

Choice of Law

This Non Disclosure Agreement shall be governed and construed in accordance with the laws of the

State of Delaware, excluding its conflicts of law provisions.

Boilerplate provisions are often overlooked as standard legal jargon, but they can have a profound impact on the enforceability and outcomes of an agreement, none more so than the choice of law clause. This clause can be the determining factor in whether a particular cause of action is recognized or enforceable under the applicable law. Far from being a mere formality, the choice-of-law clause is a cornerstone of the written agreement, crafted to bring clarity and predictability to the parties' deal.

A well-crafted choice-of-law provision is essential to maintaining the integrity of the agreement and protecting the interests of all parties involved. For this reason, choice of law clauses regularly contains the phrase "**excluding its conflicts of law provisions**". It is used so often and yet its importance is routinely overlooked and many contract administrators fail to recognize how critical the phrase is to the final agreement. The phrase "excluding its conflicts of law provisions" refers to excluding the rules that determine which law to apply when multiple jurisdictions' laws might apply due to a conflict. This ensures that the selected law governs the agreement without unintended interference from another jurisdiction's laws. This means that even if a conflict of law arises, the law of the identified state will still apply, and the court cannot use conflicts of law rules to potentially apply the law of another state.

Example Scenario

Let's say that a company in California desires to enter into a NDA with a government contractor with its principal office in New York. The California company will need to work closely with employees of the New York company whose actual offices are located in Maryland and Massachusetts. Shortly after execution of the NDA, the employees in Massachusetts are alleged to have violated the terms of the NDA and as result a formal dispute arises. Under the dispute, both California and New York have different laws that might apply, not to mention the alleged incident that occurred in Massachusetts. Without the phrase "excluding its conflicts of law provisions" phrase, the court could look at all the involved states' laws and apply the one most relevant to the individual event or case.

However, because the agreement includes a Choice of Law Clauses that reads: Choice of Law Clause: "The laws of the State of Delaware shall govern this Agreement, excluding its conflicts of law provisions", the parties have agreed that, regardless of what state's law might be "best" under a conflicts of law analysis, Delaware law will govern the agreement.

Choice of Law vs Forum Selection

Another of the often-overlooked elements of all Choice of Law clauses is a failure of the parties to not carefully consider the effects or impacts of both the Choice of Law and the Forum Selection. Forum Selection refers the location, court, place or manner in which any disputes will be resolved.

While the choice of law provision and the forum selection clause are related, they are really two distinct contractual provisions that serve different purposes. Here is an analysis of how they interact:

	Choice of Law	**Forum Selection**	**Differences**
Purpose	Specifics the State Law that will govern the interpretation, validity, and enforcement of	Designates the location (state, county, or specific court) where disputes will	What Law will be applied vs Where disputes will be resolved

	the terms of the agreement.	be litigated or arbitrated.	
SCOPE	Determines the legal framework used to resolve disputes under the agreement, such as how contract terms are interpreted or whether certain remedies are available.	Determines the venue for legal proceedings, determining where a lawsuit or arbitration must be filed.	Choice of law provisions dictate the **substantive laws** to be applied, while forum selection determines the **procedure law**, and geographical location or court system that will hear the case.
Enforceability	The chosen law can be from any jurisdiction that the parties agree to, regardless of the parties' physical locations or where the contract is executed.	Courts will generally uphold forum selection clauses unless they are unreasonable or contrary to public policy.	The choice of law can be one state, and the forum selection can be a different state.

It is important to note, and an often overlooked possibility, that the Choice of Law and the Forum Selection Clauses can specify different states. This will most often occur in situations where the parties have different preferences or in those situations where the nature of the agreement covers work that involves multiple jurisdictions. For example: A contract might specify that the laws of Delaware govern the agreement but require that disputes be litigated in a court located in Maryland.

This setup is often used when parties perceive the substantive laws of one state as more favorable but find the court system or logistical convenience of another state preferable.

When agreeing to a State Law for enforcement, it is imperative that each contractor evaluate the meaningful differences between the potential jurisdictions. The primary purpose of a Choice of Law Clause is to avoid uncertainty over the law that would govern any potential disputes, and the failure to give appropriate attention to the actual language contained in the proposal clause could result in consequences that negate the perceived benefits gained when negotiating a particular State Law for enforcement of the agreement terms.

Here is a commonly found boilerplate clause that includes Forum Selection as part of the Choice of Law Clause.

> ***Governing Law.***
>
> *This Agreement, and all claims or causes of action that may, arise out of or relate to this Agreement, the execution or performance thereof, shall be governed by, and enforced in accordance with, the laws of the State of Delaware, excluding its conflicts of law provisions and including its statutes of limitations.*

A Word About Waiver of Jury Trial

The inclusion of a waiver of trial by jury requirement in the Choice of Law is a common practice employed by many federal contractors. That is because many believe that the waiver of a trial by jury is often seen as a pragmatic way to streamline dispute resolution. By including the language within the choice of law clause, many contractors accept the requirement as "boilerplate" language and often agree that any legal disputes between the parties will be resolved by a judge, rather than a jury. While this approach can offer distinct advantages, it also carries potential risks that contractors must carefully evaluate.

The decision to waive trial by jury must be made in the context of the specific NDA or contract and the nature of the potential disputes. If the agreement involves technical or regulatory issues, a bench trial may offer the precision and efficiency needed to resolve disputes effectively. On the other hand, if disputes are likely to center on equitable issues or require compelling storytelling, retaining the right to a jury trial may provide a strategic advantage.

Ultimately, federal contractors should approach agreeing to Waive a Jury Trial with a clear understanding of all the implications, weighing the pros and cons carefully. In such a high-stakes environment, consultation with experienced legal counsel is essential to crafting a dispute resolution strategy that aligns with the contractor's goals while mitigating risks.

So what is the answer??

Well it all depends on the situation, goals, and objectives of your company.

Choosing the right language is essential for creating a predictable, enforceable, and strategically advantageous agreement and/or contract. By carefully considering these factors and tailoring the agreement to their specific needs, federal contractors can protect their interests and minimize legal uncertainties in any potential dispute.

The following sample clause is a common clause used by contractors because it addresses not only the applicable state law that will govern the agreement, but it also obligates the parties to use the state law for interpretation of any issues or disputes. Finally, this version suggests that a speedy resolution is more desirable than the potential outcome of a jury trial.

Choice of Law

This Agreement and the performance thereof shall be governed by and construed in accordance with the laws of the County of Madison, in The State of Maryland excluding its conflicts of law provisions and including its statutes of limitations. The Parties hereby irrevocably consent to the exclusive jurisdiction of the federal and/or local courts in the State of Maryland in connection with any action brought by either Party arising under or by reason of this Agreement. The parties hereby waive trial by jury with respect to any dispute relating to this agreement.

One critical point to remember is that NDAs are not governed by federal law like FAR clauses are. Instead, they are enforced under state law—and sometimes even local law. This distinction makes it essential for contractors, or their legal advisors, to understand which states have the most favorable legal interpretations and rulings when it comes to government contracting, teaming arrangements, or NDAs.

Dismissing a NDA as "just paperwork" can be a costly mistake. The reality is everything seems fine with a NDA until things go wrong. When disputes arise, the governing state's law can significantly affect how the agreement is interpreted and enforced, potentially putting one party at a severe disadvantage.

Be cautious. In federal contracting, even "small" agreements like NDAs can have significant consequences if things don't go as planned.

Companion Clauses

The Choice of Law Clause must work in harmony with the following Companion Clauses to produce an effective NDA:

Companion Clauses	**Why It's Important**
Remedies for Breach	Provides recourse if a breach occurs during the term of the NDA.
Alternative Dispute Resolutions	Outlines the mechanism by which disagreements between parties will be addressed.
Severability	Ensures that if one part of the NDA is found invalid or unenforceable, the remainder of the agreement remains intact.
Responsible Parties	Identifies individuals within the named parties who are authorized to disclose or receive information

Companion Clauses	Why It's Important
Entire Agreement	Ensures that external or prior agreements are not subject to conflicting laws or interpretations
Termination	Provides an exit mechanism for ending the NDA.

NO IMPLIED LICENSE

This clause ensures that the disclosure of information does not inadvertently grant the receiving party any rights or licenses to use the proprietary information beyond the agreed scope.

What is an Implied License?

An **implied license** arises when information or intellectual property is shared, and the receiving party assumes they have the right to use it for purposes not explicitly permitted. For example, sharing technical data, designs, or processes without clear limitations could inadvertently lead the recipient to believe they have the right to use, modify, or commercialize that information.

Why Contractors Should Be Concerned About Implied Licensing

In federal contracting, the exchange of sensitive technical data, trade secrets, and proprietary designs between contractors is a daily reality. But without the proper safeguards, this necessary collaboration can inadvertently open the door to intellectual property risks that can have far-reaching consequences.

Without an explicit "No Implied License" clause in a Non-Disclosure Agreement (NDA) or other contract, the recipient of confidential or proprietary information may attempt to assert rights they were never intended to have. This can take several dangerous forms.

First, the receiving party may claim the right to use the disclosed information in projects far beyond the original scope of the agreement. Imagine a proprietary algorithm shared for a specific government contract being used in commercial products or other ventures without permission or compensation. The potential for unauthorized use and the loss of competitive advantage are very real.

Even more insidious is the risk of modification rights. Without clear protections, the recipient may not only use the proprietary data but alter or improve it, and then claim ownership of those modifications. This could lead to the disclosing party losing control over its own intellectual property, a nightmare scenario for any business.

Perhaps the most concerning risk of all is commercialization. If the recipient is allowed to integrate the confidential information into their own products or services, they may end up competing directly with the party that originally shared the data. In an industry where intellectual property is often the key differentiator, this could be a devastating blow.

So, while the exchange of confidential information is a necessary part of doing business in the federal contracting space, it must be done with great care and foresight. A robust "No Implied License" clause is not just a best practice, it is an essential tool for protecting intellectual property, preventing unintended risks, and ensuring that collaboration does not inadvertently lead to competitive harm.

What Should a No Implied License Clause Address?

1. **Prohibit Automatic Rights:** Clearly state that the disclosure of proprietary information does not grant any licenses or rights, whether express or implied.

2. **Scope of Permissible Use:** Define the specific purposes for which the recipient is allowed to use the disclosed information.

3. **Restrictions on Use:** Prohibit unauthorized duplication, modification, or commercialization of the disclosed information.

4. **Retention of Ownership:** Affirm that the disclosing party retains full ownership of all intellectual property rights related to the disclosed information.

5. **Third-Party Sharing:** Include language that restricts the receiving party from sharing the information with third parties without prior written consent.

The following is a sample clause you can adapt for your needs:

No Implied License:

Nothing contained in this Agreement shall be construed as granting, by implication, estoppel, or otherwise, any license or rights under any patents, copyrights, trade secrets, trademarks, or other intellectual property of the Disclosing Party. The Proprietary Information provided shall only be used for the purposes expressly permitted by this Agreement and shall not be reproduced, modified, reverse-engineered, or incorporated into any products or services without the prior written consent of the Disclosing Party.

Further, nothing contained in this Non Disclosure Agreement shall grant to either party any right, title, interest, or license in or to the inventions, patents, technical data, computer software, or software documentation of the other party.

Nothing contained in this Non-Disclosure Agreement shall grant to either party the right to make commitments of any kind for or on behalf of any other party without the prior written consent of that other party..

Companion Clauses

The No Implied License Clause must work in harmony with the following Companion Clauses to produce an effective NDA:

Companion Clauses	Why It's Important
Specific Purpose	Specifies for what purposes the Confidential / Proprietary Information can and cannot be used.
Restricted Use	Ensures that only confidential, protected data is subject to use limitations.
Rights in Data	Confirms that the disclosing party retains ownership of all rights related to the confidential information
Return of Proprietary Information	Triggered at the end of the NDA's term, which begins on the Effective Date
Survivability	Extends confidentiality obligations beyond the termination of the agreement.

TERM or DURATION PERIOD

All Non-Disclosure Agreement include a clause that specifics a Period of time that the parties will remain in a contractual Relationship, this is called the "Term" or perhaps it is referred to as the "Duration Period".

Regardless of the title, this is the period of time when the parties may send, receive, or otherwise exchange confidential or proprietary information freely. Any information exchanged during the term or duration period is granted the protections under the terms of the NDA.

The second defined period covers the length of time for which confidentiality obligations are expected to apply. This is commonly referred to as the "**protection period**." Defining a protection period is crucial because confidentiality obligations typically continue after the NDA has expired or been terminated. In other words, these obligations do not automatically cease when the agreement ends or is terminated.

This discussion focuses on the Term or Duration Period only, and the concept of the protection period will be addressed in more detail in another section of this chapter.

Defining the Term or Duration

Among the many elements within an NDA, the term or duration clause addressing the time frame for exchanging information is essential. The **term or duration clause** delineates the period during which the parties are permitted to disclose information to one another in furtherance of the NDA's defined purpose. This is critical for maintaining clear boundaries and expectations. The absence of such a clause may lead to misunderstandings about when the agreement ends, leaving one or both parties vulnerable to risk.

Why the Duration of Information Exchange Matters

Scope of Engagement: Defining the term ensures that information exchange occurs only within a reasonable time frame that aligns with project milestones or the scope of discussions.

Risk Mitigation: Without a defined period for exchanging information, parties may inadvertently share sensitive data after the need for such disclosures has passed, increasing the risk of unauthorized use or legal disputes.

What the Clause Should Address

1. **Define the Disclosure Period**
   Clearly specify the start and end dates
2. **Allow for Extensions**
   Include provisions for mutual agreement to extend the period if necessary, ensuring flexibility without compromising clarity.
3. **Restrict Purpose**
   Limit disclosures strictly to the purposes defined in the NDA, ensuring information is exchanged only for agreed-upon activities.

Adapt this sample clause for your needs:

> *Duration Period*
>
> *The parties agree that the term of this Agreement shall commence on the effective date noted above and shall terminate three (3) years from that date. This period is considered the term of the agreement and is the period which proprietary information may be exchanged. Any extension of this period must be agreed upon in writing by both parties prior to its expiration.*

In the next section, we will explore the equally critical aspect of how long the information exchanged must be protected, ensuring comprehensive confidentiality safeguards.

Companion Clauses

The Term or Duration Period Clause must work in harmony with the following Companion Clauses to produce an effective NDA:

Companion Clauses	**Why It's Important**
Standards of Care	Sets clear obligations for the receiving party to protect the information shared.
Protection Period	Defines the period of time all disclosed information must be protected beyond the term or duration of the NDA.
Return of Proprietary Information	Triggered at the end of the NDA's term, which begins on the Effective Date
Remedies for Breach	Provides recourse if a breach occurs during the term of the NDA.
Information Excluded from Protection	The Standards of Care do not apply to publicly available, previously known, or independently developed information.

Companion Clauses	Why It's Important
Termination	Provides an exit mechanism for ending the NDA.
Survivability	Extends confidentiality obligations beyond the termination of the agreement.

PROTECTION PERIOD

This clause defines how long the receiving party must protect disclosed information from unauthorized use or disclosure, extending beyond the term of the agreement. While often overlooked, this provision offers significant benefits for both parties and demands careful attention during drafting and negotiation.

Understanding the Protection Period

The **protection period** is distinct from the term or duration of the NDA, which governs how long parties may exchange information under the agreement. Instead, the protection period begins at disclosure and specifies the timeframe during which the receiving party is obligated to safeguard the disclosed information.

This clause ensures that proprietary or sensitive data remains protected, even after the NDA's formal term expires, aligning with the practical needs of long-term government contracts.

The Time Factor: Why Defining the Protection Period is Crucial

So why should contractors be concerned about the length of protection period? The answer lies in the potential consequences of an improperly defined or overly restrictive timeline.

On one hand, a NDA with too short a protection period may leave sensitive information exposed. If the agreement expires before the confidential data has lost its value or relevance, the disclosing party may find itself without recourse should the recipient misuse or disclose that information. This is particularly concerning for industries where technological advancements occur slowly, allowing information to remain valuable for an extended period. A protection period that is too brief may not provide sufficient protection for the lifespan of the data.

On the other hand, a NDA with too long of a protection period or one that requires indefinite confidentiality can be overly burdensome on the recipient. It may limit their ability to use information that has become publicly available or no longer holds competitive value. This could not only create unnecessary restrictions but also make the recipient less likely to enter into the agreement in the first place, potentially stifling collaboration and innovation.

Key Considerations for Determining Appropriate Protection Periods

- **Industry Standards**: While the ideal term can vary depending on the nature of the information being shared, 3 to 5 years is generally accepted as the industry standard for most NDAs. However, for highly specialized technical information, longer protection periods may be necessary.

- **Context dependence**: The duration of the NDA should be tied to the useful life of the confidential information. Data that remains valuable for an extended period should have a longer protection period, while information with a shorter shelf life may require a shorter term.

- **Negotiation**: The term and duration should be open to negotiation based on the specific needs and risks of the parties involved. Contractors should carefully consider what they are comfortable with and what will provide adequate protection without being overly restrictive.

- **Establish the Required Tracking Systems**
  Implement tools or processes to monitor disclosure dates and protection timelines (if needed for compliance).

- **Avoid Administrative Pitfalls**: While starting the protection period at disclosure offers advantages, ensure the system in place can handle the tracking complexities.

Consider the following as a potential clause

Protection Period:

The period of performance regarding mutual protection of Proprietary Information survives the expiration or termination date of this Non-Disclosure Agreement for a period of three (3) years, or such period until the information falls into the public domain, or until such time the information has been returned or destroyed in accordance with the clause entitled Return or Destruction of Protected Information. During the protection period the receiving party shall safeguard and hold in strict confidence such proprietary Information and prevent disclosure thereof to third parties, without the written consent of the disclosing party. The receiving party shall further restrict the disclosure of such Proprietary Information to only those employees who have a need to know. During the above-mentioned protection period, no other use of the Proprietary Information is granted without the written consent of the Disclosing Party.

Here is a second option for your consideration:

Protection Period:

Regardless of the date information has been disclosed the recipient agrees to maintain, protect and prevent disclosure to unauthorized parties for a period of three (3) years following the last date of the term, or date of termination, of this Agreement. This additional two-year period is considered the protection period. During the protection period the receiving party shall safeguard and hold in strict confidence such proprietary Information and prevent disclosure thereof to third parties, without the written consent of the disclosing party. The receiving party shall further restrict the disclosure of such Proprietary Information to only those employees who have a need to know. During the above-mentioned protection period, no other use of the Proprietary Information is granted without the written consent of the Disclosing Party.

By clearly defining this period, contractors can achieve a balance between robust confidentiality and manageable obligations, benefiting both parties involved. A well-crafted protection period clause demonstrates professionalism, mitigates risks, and ensures compliance in the complex world of government contracts. For contractors, understanding and negotiating this clause is an indispensable part of securing their competitive edge.

Companion Clauses

The Protection Period Clause must work in harmony with the following Companion Clauses to produce an effective NDA:

Companion Clauses	**Why It's Important**
Survivability	Extends confidentiality obligations beyond the termination of the agreement.
Return of Proprietary Information	Ensures information is removed after the protection period ends.

Companion Clauses	Why It's Important
Standards of Care	Sets clear obligations for the receiving party to protect the information shared.
Remedies for Breach	Provides recourse if a breach occurs during the term of the NDA.
Exclusions from Confidential Information	Clarifies what is not protected during the period.
Permitted Disclosure	Allows disclosures under defined circumstances.
Term or Duration Period	Works directly with the Effective Date to define when the NDA starts and how long confidentiality obligations remain in effect.
Termination	Provides an exit mechanism for ending the NDA.

AFFILIATES AND THIRD PARTIES

One of the most consistently debated clauses of NDAs is ensuring that the disclosing party's proprietary information is not shared with affiliates, agents, subcontractors, representatives, consultants, auditors, or any other third parties without explicit control and safeguards and the written consent of the Disclosing Party. Allowing broad access to sensitive information introduces significant risks, ranging from potential misuse to diminished enforceability of the NDA itself.

Why Should Contractors Care About Disclosure to Affiliates and Third Parties?

At the heart of this issue is control. When a receiving party is allowed to disclose proprietary information to affiliates, agents, or other third parties, the disclosing party loses a significant degree of control over who has access to its sensitive information. Affiliates, for instance, may include a range of entities over which the receiving party has influence or control, creating a broader network of access than intended.

Affiliates are defined as entities where one company controls or has the power to control another, or a third party has the power to control both. This interconnectedness can pose substantial risks. For example, affiliates might not operate under the same confidentiality standards or may be located in jurisdictions with weaker data protection laws, increasing the chances of unintentional disclosures.

Additionally, allowing such disclosures opens the door for misuse by subcontractors, consultants, or auditors who may lack a vested interest in safeguarding the disclosing party's proprietary information. Without stringent controls, the risk of intellectual property theft, regulatory violations, or competitive disadvantage increases dramatically.

What Contractors Gain by Limiting Disclosure

Contractors that prevent their proprietary information from being shared with affiliates or third parties gain significant advantages. First, they maintain tighter control over who has access to sensitive data, reducing the risk of misuse, unintentional leaks, or exposure to competitors.

Second, this limitation ensures accountability. If proprietary information is disclosed only to parties with explicit approval, the disclosing party can hold the receiving party directly responsible for any breaches. This clarity strengthens the NDA's enforceability and provides greater legal recourse in the event of a violation.

Finally, limiting disclosure fosters transparency. It forces the receiving party to disclose any intended third-party recipients upfront, allowing the disclosing party to evaluate these entities during the due diligence phase. This proactive approach can prevent misunderstandings and ensure all parties are aligned on the scope of information sharing.

What Should the Clause Address?

An effective clause restricting disclosure to affiliates, agents, and third parties should:

1. **Prohibit Blanket Disclosures:** Prevent the receiving party from automatically sharing proprietary information with affiliates, subcontractors, consultants, or auditors without explicit written approval.
2. **Require Written Notification and Consent:** The clause should mandate that the receiving party provide a written explanation of any third party's involvement, including the necessity of their access and the protective measures (e.g., firewalls) in place.

3. **Mandate Individual NDAs:** Require that any third-party receiving access sign a separate NDA directly with the disclosing party.
4. **Accept Full Legal Liability:** The receiving party must accept full liability for any actions or breaches committed by affiliates, agents, or other third parties.
5. **Establish a Limited List of Approved Entities:** If references to third parties cannot be removed, the NDA should list specific entities allowed access, including their contact information, and prohibit disclosure to any other parties.

This clause may serve as a useful example for your purposes.

Third-Party Disclosure Restrictions Clause:

"The Receiving Party shall not disclose the Disclosing Party's proprietary information to any affiliates, agents, subcontractors, representatives, consultants, auditors, or any other third parties without the prior written consent of the Disclosing Party. If such disclosure is permitted, the Receiving Party shall provide a written explanation detailing the necessity of access and the protective measures in place to safeguard the Disclosing Party's information. The Receiving Party must ensure that each third party has executed a separate NDA directly with the Disclosing Party prior to gaining access to any proprietary information. The Receiving Party agrees to accept full legal liability for any actions, breaches, or misuse of proprietary information by affiliates, agents, subcontractors, representatives, consultants, auditors, or third parties.

Optional additional Paragraph to be used when references to third parties cannot be removed:

After meeting the above stated requirements, the receiving party may share the disclosing party's confidential or proprietary information with only those affiliates, agents, subcontractors, representatives, consultants, auditors, or other third parties listed below. Under no circumstance or situation shall the disclosing party's confidential or proprietary information be disclosed to entities not listed in the table below without the express written consent of the Disclosing Party.

Entity Identification	Full Address	POC Name & Title	Email and Phone

Managing Negotiations and Alternatives

During negotiations, contractors should strive to remove any references to affiliates, agents, representatives, or third parties from NDAs. If this is not feasible, requiring individual NDAs with each entity or listing the specific parties permitted to access information can mitigate risks. Additionally, contractors should insist on written notification requirements whenever affiliates or third parties gain access to their proprietary information.

A recommended compromise is to allow disclosure only to explicitly listed entities, with the receiving party accepting full liability for their actions. For example, a table within the NDA can identify approved entities, including their names, addresses, and contact details, ensuring transparency and traceability.

Legal Liabilities and Remedies

In cases where affiliates, agents, or third parties misuse proprietary information, the disclosing party must have robust legal recourse. The NDA should provide for remedies such as indemnification, monetary damages, and injunctive relief to prevent further misuse. By holding the receiving party accountable for the actions of third parties, the disclosing party strengthens its position and reduces the likelihood of disputes.

Preventing disclosure to affiliates, agents, and third parties is not only a best practice but a necessity for ensuring the integrity of NDAs. By incorporating stringent restrictions, requiring individual NDAs, and enforcing full liability, contractors can protect their sensitive data while fostering trust and accountability

Companion Clauses

The Affiliates and Third Parties Clause must work in harmony with the following Companion Clauses to produce an effective NDA:

Companion Clauses	Why It's Important
Standards of Care	Sets clear obligations for the receiving party to protect the information shared.
Specific Purpose	Specifies for what purposes the Confidential / Proprietary Information can and cannot be used.
Assignment	Prevents parties from transferring their obligations under the NDA to third parties without consent.

Companion Clauses	Why It's Important
Restricted Use	Ensures that only confidential, protected data is subject to use limitations.
Permitted Disclosure	Allows disclosures under defined circumstances.
Notice of Breach	Requires the receiving party to promptly notify the disclosing party if covered information is disclosed or mishandled.
Remedies for Breach	Provides recourse if a breach occurs during the term of the NDA.
Return of Proprietary Information	Ensures confidential information is returned or destroyed when the NDA ends.
Survivability	Extends confidentiality obligations beyond the termination of the agreement.
Termination	Provides an exit mechanism for ending the NDA.

RESTRICTED USE

A frequently underestimated but crucial provision within Non-Disclosure Agreements is the Restricted Use Clause. This clause limits the use of disclosed information strictly to the purpose explicitly stated in the NDA, plays a key role in preventing misuse, reverse engineering, or unintended repurposing of proprietary data.

Why Restricting Use is Critical

Restricting the use of proprietary information to the specific purpose defined in the NDA is vital for several reasons. First and foremost, failure to include such restrictions can inadvertently result in a **general disclosure**, effectively waiving the confidentiality protections of the NDA. Without explicit limitations, the receiving party may interpret the absence of restrictions as permission to use the data broadly, including for unrelated projects or programs.

By restricting use, the disclosing party ensures that the receiving party cannot manipulate the data, reverse-engineer it, or derive new insights from it that could be leveraged for other efforts. This safeguard is particularly important in the competitive landscape of government contracting, where even minor misuse of data could lead to significant commercial or strategic disadvantages.

Furthermore, restricting use enhances the enforceability of the NDA. Courts are more likely to uphold the agreement's terms if the use of information is clearly confined to a specific purpose. This clarity also simplifies dispute resolution by providing a well-defined standard against which compliance can be measured.

What Contractors Gain by Restricting Use

Contractors that include a Purpose Limitation Clause in their NDAs benefit because they maintain greater control over their proprietary information, ensuring it is only used in furtherance of the specific initiative for which it was shared, such as teaming agreements or proposal submissions.

Also, such a clause reduces the risk of competitive harm. By prohibiting the receiving party from using the information for unrelated purposes, the disclosing party minimizes the chances of their data being repurposed to benefit competitors or other programs.

Finally, restricting use reinforces trust and accountability between parties. It demonstrates that the disclosing party values the integrity of the agreement and expects the receiving party to act in good faith. This mutual understanding is essential for fostering long-term business relationships.

Key Terms of an Effective Clause

A well-drafted Purpose Limitation Clause should address the following:

1. **Specificity of Purpose:** The clause must define the exact purpose for which the information is being shared, such as exploring a potential teaming agreement or preparing a proposal for a specific solicitation or contract.

2. **Prohibited Actions:** The clause should explicitly prohibit the receiving party from manipulating the data, reverse-engineering it, or deriving secondary insights from it.

3. **Restricted Scope:** The clause should ensure the data is used exclusively for the identified purposes and not for any unrelated programs, projects, or competitive activities.

4. **Legal Liability:** The receiving party must accept full liability for any misuse of the information, including unauthorized use by their employees or third parties.

5. **Remedies for Breach:** The clause should outline the remedies available to the disclosing party in case of a breach, including injunctive relief, monetary damages, and indemnification.

Below is an example clause for your reference

Restricted Use Clause:

The Receiving Party agrees that any proprietary information disclosed by the Disclosing Party under this Agreement shall be used solely for the specific purpose stated elsewhere in this agreement. The Receiving Party shall not use the disclosed information for any other purpose, including but not limited to reverse engineering, deriving secondary data, or applying the information to unrelated programs or initiatives. By executing this agreement, the Receiving Party accepts full legal liability for any unauthorized use of the disclosed information, whether by itself or its employees, affiliates, consultants, agents, subcontractors or third parties. In the event of a breach, the rights of the parties to seek injunctive relief, monetary damages, and full indemnification for any losses incurred will be consistent with the clause entitled "Available Remedies". This clause shall survive the termination of this agreement.

Legal Liabilities and Remedies

When the Purpose Limitation Clause is breached, the disclosing party must have clear legal remedies available. These should include the right to seek **injunctive relief**, preventing the receiving party from further misuse of the information. Monetary damages should also be specified to compensate the disclosing party for any financial harm caused by the breach. Additionally, indemnification clauses can ensure that the receiving party bears the full cost of any legal or regulatory consequences stemming from their actions.

Recommendations for Best Practices

To maximize the effectiveness of a Restricted Use Clause, contractors should ensure the following:

- **Precise Language:** Clearly define the purpose and prohibit any actions beyond that scope. A Clearly defined purpose will indicate a potential contract name, maybe a contract or solicitation number. The more detailed information contained in the description of the purpose, the greater leverage the disclosing party has as protection. Even the slightest hint of ambiguity will weaken the enforceability of the NDA.

- **Due Diligence:** Before entering into the agreement, confirm that the receiving party understands and accepts the restrictions.

- **Enforcement Mechanisms:** Regularly monitor the use of disclosed information and be prepared to take swift action in case of a suspected breach.

- **Complementary Clauses:** Pair the Restricted Use Clause with other protective measures, such as restrictions on disclosure to affiliates or third parties, to create a comprehensive safeguard.

Restricting the use of disclosed information to a specific purpose is not just advisable, it is essential. A Restricted Use Clause ensures that sensitive data is used only for its intended purpose, allows contractors a mechanism to protect their interests, and enhances the enforceability of the agreement.

Companion Clauses

The Restricted Use Clause must work in harmony with the following Companion Clauses to produce an effective NDA:

Companion Clauses	Why It's Important
Specific Purpose	Specifies for what purposes the Confidential / Proprietary Information can and cannot be used.
Standards of Care	Sets clear obligations for the receiving party to protect the information shared.
No Implied License	Prohibits the recipient of confidential or proprietary information from attempting to assert rights they were never intended to have.
Affiliates and Third Parties	Ensures that any third parties or affiliates granted access to the confidential information are also required to adhere to the Standards of Care
Return of Proprietary Information	Ensures confidential information is returned or destroyed when the NDA ends.

Companion Clauses	Why It's Important
Remedies for Breach	Provides recourse if a breach occurs during the term of the NDA.
Survivability	Extends confidentiality obligations beyond the termination of the agreement.

RIGHTS IN DATA

While NDAs often focus on confidentiality and use restrictions, including a "Rights in Data" clause is equally critical. This clause defines how data—such as technical information, intellectual property, or work products—will be treated, owned, and used during and after the contractual relationship. For contractors and their government clients, the stakes are high: clearly addressing rights in data ensures that intellectual property is safeguarded, responsibilities are clear, and disputes are minimized.

Why Include a "Rights in Data" Clause?

1. Clear Ownership and Usage Rights

A well-drafted Rights in Data clause specifies who owns the data created, shared, or developed under the contract. This clarity is critical for contractors who need to protect their proprietary technologies or methodologies while complying with government requirements. For government clients, such clauses ensure access to necessary data without overstepping intellectual property boundaries.

2. Avoiding Future Disputes

Without a Rights in Data clause, disagreements about ownership, use, or access rights can arise, potentially leading to litigation. By addressing these issues upfront, both parties avoid ambiguity and establish a mutual understanding of their rights and obligations.

3. Compliance with Regulations

For government contracts, compliance with Federal Acquisition Regulation (FAR) and Defense FAR Supplement (DFARS) clauses related to data rights is non-negotiable.

Including a Rights in Data clause tailored to these regulations helps contractors align with legal and contractual obligations, avoiding penalties or disputes.

4. Preserving Competitive Advantage

For contractors, a well-crafted clause can protect sensitive data, ensuring it is not improperly disclosed or misused. This is particularly critical when the data involves trade secrets, technical designs, or other proprietary information.

Are Rights in Data Concerns Appropriate for NDAs?

A Rights in Data clause is likely unnecessary in an NDA, which focuses solely on confidentiality and does not govern ownership, licensing, or the creation of intellectual property. Teaming Agreements are designed for joint efforts between parties pursuing a government contract. These agreements often involve significant collaboration, including:

1. **Creation of Work Products**: Parties may jointly develop proposals, designs, or technical solutions requiring clear definitions of data ownership and rights.
2. **Sharing of Pre-Existing Intellectual Property**: Proprietary methodologies, software, or technical data may need to be shared to enable effective collaboration.
3. **Data Usage and Licensing**: Teaming Agreements often address how shared or jointly developed data can be used, both during and after the agreement's term.

Given these elements, a Rights in Data clause is crucial in a Teaming Agreement where the sharing, creation, and ownership of data are integral to the collaboration, rather than NDAs, which focus narrowly on confidentiality.

Key Considerations for the Rights in Data Clause

An effective Rights in Data clause should address the following key elements:

1. Data Ownership
The clause should clearly define who owns the data. For example:
- Government Purpose Rights: Specifies that the government can use the data for specific purposes but does not gain ownership.
- Unlimited Rights: Grants the government complete ownership and use rights.
- Contractor-Owned Data: Ensures that proprietary data developed before or outside the contract remains the contractor's property.

2. Scope of Use
Specify how the data can be used by the receiving party. For instance:
- Allow government use for internal purposes only.
- Prohibit disclosure to third parties without prior approval.

3. Restrictions on Reproduction and Distribution
The clause should limit how the data can be copied or distributed, safeguarding proprietary and sensitive information.

4. Data Marking Requirements
To enforce rights, contractors must properly mark proprietary data. The clause should specify that unmarked data may be deemed government-owned or public domain, depending on the circumstances.

5. Duration of Rights
Define the timeframe for data rights, ensuring proprietary protections extend beyond the contract period if necessary.

6. Remedies for Breach

The clause should specify remedies for unauthorized use or disclosure, such as injunctive relief, damages, or termination of access rights.

Why Contractors and Government Clients Should Care

Both parties benefit from a well-crafted Rights in Data clause. Contractors gain protection for their intellectual property, ensuring that proprietary innovations are not misappropriated or publicly disclosed. Government clients, on the other hand, secure access to critical data necessary for contract execution and continuity of operations. Without such clarity, disputes over data use, access, or ownership can hinder project progress and lead to costly legal battles.

Legal Liabilities and Remedies

The absence of a Rights in Data clause or its improper drafting can lead to:

1. Breach of Contract: Unauthorized use or disclosure of data could result in contractual penalties or litigation.
2. Loss of Competitive Advantage: Contractors risk losing control over proprietary innovations or methodologies.
3. Government Compliance Risks: Non-compliance with FAR or DFARS data requirements could result in penalties or loss of contract.

Remedies for violations may include:

- **Injunctive Relief:** Preventing further unauthorized use or disclosure.
- **Compensatory Damages:** Reimbursement for losses incurred due to misuse.

- **Termination:** Cancellation of the contract for material breaches.

Example Industry Standard Clause

> ***Rights in Data:***
> *All technical data, software, and related deliverables developed or provided under this Agreement shall be subject to the following terms: All technical data, software, and related deliverables developed or provided under this Agreement shall be subject to the following terms: (a) Proprietary data disclosed and marked as such shall remain the sole property of the Disclosing Party and shall not be disclosed or used by the Government except for purposes expressly authorized under this Agreement. (b) The Government shall have Government Purpose Rights to all data developed exclusively for this Agreement, allowing use, reproduction, and modification for government purposes only. (c) The disclosing Party shall provide all deliverables with appropriate data markings in compliance with FAR 52.227-14 and DFARS 252.227-7013. Any unmarked data shall be deemed to fall under Unlimited Rights. (d) Unauthorized use or disclosure of proprietary data shall entitle the Disclosing Party to injunctive relief, damages, and any other remedies available under applicable law.*

A Rights in Data clause protects contractors' innovations while ensuring government clients can fulfill their mission-critical needs. By addressing ownership, use, restrictions, and remedies, contractors and government entities can avoid disputes, protect their interests, and ensure compliance with legal and contractual obligations.

Companion Clauses

The Rights in Data Clause must work in harmony with the following Companion Clauses to produce an effective NDA:

Companion Clauses	Why It's Important
Definitions	Ensures clarity on what qualifies as "data" or "information" under the agreement.
Specific Purpose	Specifies for what purposes the Confidential / Proprietary Information can and cannot be used.
Assignment	Prevents parties from transferring their obligations under the NDA to third parties without consent.
Restricted Use	Ensures that only confidential, protected data is subject to use limitations.
Return of Proprietary Information	Ensures confidential information is returned or destroyed when the NDA ends.
Warranties	May include assurances that the data shared is owned by the disclosing party and that no third party rights are being violated.
Remedies for Breach	Provides recourse if a breach occurs during the term of the NDA.

Companion Clauses	Why It's Important
No Implied License	Prohibits the recipient of confidential or proprietary information from attempting to assert rights they were never intended to have.
Alternative Dispute Resolutions	Outlines the mechanism by which disagreements between parties will be addressed.
Liquidated Damages	Predefines the financial consequences of failing to protect the disclosing party's confidential information
Choice of Law	Specifies the legal framework and venue for resolving disputes.
Survivability	Extends confidentiality obligations beyond the termination of the agreement.

REMEDIES FOR BREACH

The **Remedies Clause** outlines the consequences of breaching confidentiality and ensures enforceability through appropriate legal means. When paired with a governing law clause and litigation as the resolution method, the Remedies Clause provides clarity, enforceability, and protection for contracting parties.

Why the Remedies Clause Matters

The Remedies Clause is vital because it serves multiple purposes. First, it acts as a deterrent by clearly defining the consequences of a breach thereby discouraging parties from violating confidentiality obligations. Second, it provides clarity by specifying what constitutes a breach and the associated remedies, which reduces the potential ambiguities. Third, it facilitates enforcement by granting courts a clear basis to impose appropriate penalties. Finally, it protects the business interests of both parties by addressing potential damages or injunctions, thereby minimizing the harm caused by a breach.

Key Elements of a Remedies Clause

A well-drafted Remedies Clause in a NDA should include several critical components:

1. **Acknowledgment of Care Standards**:
   It is common to include a provision stating that neither party will be held liable for inadvertent or accidental disclosure of proprietary information, provided they exercised the same degree of care they use to protect their own information. This ensures fairness and reasonableness in assessing liability.

2. **Recognition of Non-Monetary Remedies**:
   The clause should acknowledge that monetary damages may not always be sufficient to remedy a breach. For example, a NDA might state that a breach could cause irreparable harm and that the injured party may seek injunctive relief in addition to monetary damages.

3. **Specification of Penalties**:
   The clause should clearly outline the financial consequences of a breach, including potential liability for attorney's fees, court costs, and other expenses incurred in enforcing the agreement. This helps set expectations for the financial impact of a breach.

4. **Types of Remedies**:
   Remedies may include injunctive relief to prevent further breaches, liquidated damages for pre-estimated harm, or actual damages to compensate for losses.

What to Avoid

1. **Ambiguous or Broad Language**:
   Avoid overly vague phrases such as "reasonable remedies," which can lead to disputes over interpretation.
2. **Excessive Penalties**:
   Remedies should be proportional to the breach to avoid challenges to enforceability.
3. **Conflicting Clauses**:
   Avoid including arbitration or mediation as alternate remedies if the governing law clause specifies litigation.

Concerns and Issues to Address

One of the primary concerns in drafting a Remedies Clause is defining financial liability. Many parties resist including provisions that require reimbursement of attorney's fees, court costs, or other expenses, arguing that these terms can lead to excessive financial burdens. Another concern is the scope of injunctive relief, as courts may impose limits if the NDA does not provide clear and specific language regarding the necessity of such relief. Furthermore, enforceability can become an issue if the clause conflicts with the governing law or is not supported by the selected jurisdiction. It is also critical to address whether remedies and confidentiality obligations survive the termination of the NDA, as breaches discovered after termination may otherwise go unremedied.

Example of an Industry-Standard Remedies Clause

> ***Available Remedies:*** *Both parties acknowledge that unauthorized use or disclosure of the Proprietary Information could cause irreparable harm and significant injury to the other party, for which monetary damages may not be a sufficient remedy. Accordingly, any controversy, dispute, or claim arising out of or related to this Agreement, including any breach thereof and issues that cannot be resolved thru mutual negotiation, shall be resolved through litigation.*
>
> *Both parties agree that the non-breaching party shall be entitled, without waving any other rights or remedies, to seek, without bond, equitable relief, including injunctions, to prevent unauthorized use or disclosure of Proprietary Information. Provided that the court finds that a breach occurred, the breaching party shall be liable and shall pay to the non-breaching party all reasonable costs and fees, including, but not limited to, attorney's fees and court costs, incurred by such non-breaching party in connection with such litigation, including any appeal therefrom. This clause shall survive termination of the Agreement.*

When paired with a governing law clause and litigation, it ensures robust protection and enforceability. By including specific provisions for care standards, remedies, and financial penalties, contractors can safeguard their interests while maintaining trust and clarity in contractual relationships.

Companion Clauses

The Remedies for Breach Clause must work in harmony with the following Companion Clauses to produce an effective NDA:

Companion Clauses	Why It's Important
Choice of Law	Specifies the legal framework and venue for resolving disputes.
Notice of Breach	Requires the receiving party to promptly notify the disclosing party if covered information is disclosed or mishandled.
Alternative Dispute Resolutions	Outlines the mechanism by which disagreements between parties will be addressed.
Liquidated Damages	Predefines the financial consequences of failing to protect the disclosing party's confidential information
Survivability	Extends confidentiality obligations beyond the termination of the agreement.
Termination	Provides an exit mechanism for ending the NDA.

ALTERNATIVE DISPUTE RESOLUTIONS

An Alternative Dispute Resolution (ADR) Clause outlines the mechanism by which disagreements between parties will be addressed, offering clarity and direction when disputes arise. The key question in resolving disputes is whether they should be handled in court or through an alternative method known as ADR. ADR serves as a broad category encompassing various techniques (such as mediation, arbitration, and negotiation) for resolving disagreements outside of formal court proceedings. It is widely recognized as a practical and efficient "Plan B" for addressing conflicts and firms are convinced that ADR offers faster, less expensive, and less stressful alternatives to traditional litigation.

Rather than relying on a judge and jury in a formal trial, ADR methods provide flexible approaches to conflict resolution. These methods are designed to simplify the process while maintaining fairness and effectiveness. ADR typically includes four main methods:

1. **Mediation**: Mediation involves a neutral third party who acts as a referee, helping both sides have a constructive conversation. The mediator does not make decisions but facilitates discussions to help the parties find common ground and reach an agreement.

2. **Arbitration**: Arbitration is similar to hiring a private judge. Both parties present their case to an impartial arbitrator who makes a binding decision. While less formal than court, arbitration provides a structured and enforceable resolution.

3. **Negotiation**: Negotiation is the simplest form of ADR, where the parties involved—often with the assistance of their attorneys—sit down to discuss and reach a mutually agreeable solution through compromise.

Why Include an Alternative Dispute Resolution Clause?

Disputes are an inevitable part of business relationships, and a well-crafted clause is a proactive step that benefits all parties by fostering clarity, reducing costs, preserving relationships, and supporting effective risk management.

One of the primary advantages is **preemptive clarity**. By explicitly defining how disputes will be resolved, the clause reduces ambiguity and helps the parties save time and resources during conflicts. Knowing the agreed-upon method for resolution eliminates confusion and sets expectations in advance.

Another key benefit is **cost efficiency**. The chosen resolution process can significantly impact costs. For example, methods like negotiation or mediation are typically far more cost-effective than pursuing litigation, which is often lengthy and expensive.

The clause also promotes the **preservation of relationships**. Collaborative methods such as mediation and negotiation encourage cooperation and are less adversarial than litigation, which can strain or even sever professional relationships. This is particularly important in long-term or strategic partnerships.

Lastly, a dispute resolution clause enhances **predictability and risk management**. By outlining the resolution process, contractors can better anticipate costs, timelines, and potential outcomes. This predictability enables more effective planning and minimizes the uncertainties associated with unresolved disputes.

Incorporating a dispute resolution clause is a proactive step that benefits all parties by fostering clarity, reducing costs, preserving relationships, and supporting effective risk management.

Analysis of Potential Dispute Resolution Methods

1. **Court Litigation**
   Description: Court is suitable for setting legal precedents or resolving complex disputes involving third parties or public interest. It is the traditional and formal process of resolving disputes through the judicial system. It involves filing a lawsuit, adhering to strict procedural rules, presenting evidence before a judge (and potentially a jury), and obtaining a binding judgment. This process is governed by the laws of the jurisdiction where the lawsuit is filed and often involves multiple stages, including pre-trial motions, discovery, trial, and the possibility of appeal.

Advantages:
   1. Binding and Enforceable Outcomes: Decisions made by a court are legally binding and backed by the full authority of the judicial system.
   2. Precedent Setting: Court rulings can establish legal precedents, providing clarity for future cases.
   3. Comprehensive Process: The court system allows for extensive discovery, evidence presentation, and cross-examination, ensuring thorough examination of the dispute.
   4. Public Accountability: Court proceedings are part of the public record, promoting transparency in certain types of disputes, such as those involving public funds or public interest.
   5. Appeal Rights: Litigants have the right to appeal decisions, offering additional safeguards against errors or unfair judgments.

   Industry Standard Clause
   Any dispute, controversy, or claim arising out of or relating to this Agreement, including any breach thereof, shall be resolved through litigation in the

courts of [Jurisdiction]. Each party irrevocably submits to the exclusive jurisdiction of the courts of [Jurisdiction] and agrees that venue for any litigation shall lie in [City, State]. The prevailing party shall be entitled to recover reasonable attorney's fees, court costs, and any other expenses incurred in the enforcement of this Agreement.

2. **Mediation**:
   Description: A neutral third party facilitates a discussion to help reach a mutually agreeable solution.

   Advantages: Non-binding, preserves relationships, cost-effective. Works for parties seeking an amicable resolution.

   Industry Standard Clause:
   Any dispute arising out of or related to this Agreement shall first be subject to mediation by a mutually agreed mediator. The mediation shall occur within 30 days of written notice of dispute.

3. **Arbitration**:
   Description: Parties present their case to an arbitrator, whose decision is typically binding.

   Advantages: Confidential, expert arbitrators, enforceable decisions. Effective for disputes requiring industry-specific expertise and confidentiality.

   Industry Standard Clause - Basic:
   All disputes arising from this Agreement shall be resolved by arbitration conducted under the rules of the [Arbitration Institution], and the decision shall be binding and enforceable in any competent court.

4. **Negotiation**:
   Description: Direct discussion between parties to reach a resolution.

   Advantages: Informal, quick, cost-effective, preserves control. Offers the greatest flexibility and lowest costs for less complex disagreements.

   > ***Industry Standard Clause:***
   > *The parties agree to meet and negotiate in good faith to resolve any disputes arising under this Agreement before initiating any other dispute resolution process.*

Comparison of Dispute Resolution Methods

The table below provides an overview of the primary dispute resolution processes, comparing them across key criteria to help identify the most advantageous method for resolving disputes.

Criteria	Court Litigation	Arbitration	Mediation	Negotiation
Time to Resolution	1-3+ years	3-12 months	1-3 months	2 weeks-2 months
Cost	$$$$$	$$$	$$	$
Privacy	Public record	Private	Private	Private
Control Over Outcome	Low (judge decides)	Medium (arbitrator decides)	High (parties decide)	High (parties decide)

Criteria	Court Litigation	Arbitration	Mediation	Negotiation
Formality Level	Very formal	Semi-formal	Informal	Informal
Binding Nature	Binding	Usually binding	Non-binding	Binding if agreed
Expert Knowledge	Judge may lack industry expertise	Arbitrator chosen for expertise	Mediator chosen for expertise	Direct knowledge of parties
Precedent Value	Creates legal precedent	Limited precedent	No precedent	No precedent
Flexibility of Process	Rigid, formal rules	Somewhat flexible	Very flexible	Highly flexible
Cost Predictability	Low	Medium	High	High
Enforceability	Strong	Strong	Depends on agreement	Depends on agreement

Choosing the Right Dispute Resolution Method:

When disputes arise, the chosen resolution method can significantly impact costs, time, relationships, and outcomes. Each approach—court litigation, arbitration, mediation, or direct negotiation—comes with its own set of perceived drawbacks and actual benefits. The following table breaks down why companies might hesitate to use each method and highlights the unique advantages they offer. This side-by-side comparison provides valuable insights for making informed decisions in navigating conflict resolution.

Method	Why Companies Avoid It	Why It's Actually Valuable
Court Litigation	• Expensive discovery process • Public record risks exposing trade secrets • Length of process (2-5 years average) • Unpredictable judges/juries who may not understand technical aspects • Risk of precedent-setting decisions • Destroys business relationships	• Clear appeals process • Ability to set legal precedents when desired • Power to compel evidence/testimony • Familiar process for legal teams • Strong enforcement mechanisms • Can be necessary for constitutional/statutory issues
Arbitration	• Still relatively expensive • Limited appeals process • Risk of "split the baby" decisions • Can be almost as formal as litigation • Hard to challenge biased arbitrators • Increasing costs	• Private proceedings protect sensitive info • Can select arbitrators with technical/industry expertise • Faster than litigation (8-12 months) • More flexible procedures than court • Enforceable internationally

Method	Why Companies Avoid It	Why It's Actually Valuable
	approaching litigation levels	• Limited discovery reduces costs
Mediation	• Viewed as "soft" approach • No guaranteed resolution • Requires both parties to compromise • Depends heavily on mediator skill • Can be used as delay tactic • May reveal strategy if litigation follows	• Preserves business relationships • Fastest resolution (1-3 months) • Lowest cost option • Parties control outcome • Completely confidential • Can address non-legal issues • Creative solutions possible
Direct Negotiation	• Power imbalances affect outcomes • No neutral third party guidance • May be seen as admission of weakness • Requires trust between parties • Limited enforcement mechanisms • Success depends on negotiation skills	• Lowest cost (internal resources only) • Maximum control over process • Fastest when successful • Completely private • Maintains direct communication • Preserves relationships • Can be very informal

Now that we've examined the pros and cons of various dispute resolution methods, let's delve into a practical application by exploring a standard arbitration clause commonly used in government contracts. Here is a Standard Arbitration Clause for a Government Contract that you may consider to your use:

Arbitration Clause:
Any dispute, controversy, or claim arising out of or relating to this contract, including the breach, termination, or validity thereof, shall be resolved by arbitration administered by [Designated Arbitration Institution, e.g., the American Arbitration Association] in accordance with its [specific rules, e.g., Commercial Arbitration Rules]. The arbitration shall be conducted in the English language, and the place of arbitration shall be [City, State]. The arbitral tribunal shall consist of [one/three] arbitrator(s), appointed in accordance with the applicable rules. The arbitrator(s) shall have experience in government contracting and shall issue a written decision stating the reasons for the award. The decision of the arbitrator(s) shall be final and binding upon the parties, and judgment on the award rendered by the arbitrator(s) may be entered in any court of competent jurisdiction. Each party shall bear its own costs and expenses associated with the arbitration, except as otherwise determined by the arbitrator(s).

Notwithstanding the foregoing, either party may seek interim or injunctive relief from a court of competent jurisdiction to protect its rights or property pending the resolution of the arbitration.

This arbitration clause offers a structured and enforceable framework for resolving disputes while allowing flexibility and supporting the preservation of professional relationships. The clause explicitly designates a place of arbitration and specifies the use of a tribunal format for the proceedings. However, it lacks a critical element: the governing law to be applied during the arbitration.

Omitting a governing law from an arbitration clause can lead to several challenges. Without a clearly defined legal framework, arbitrators or courts must determine which jurisdiction's laws apply to the contract and its disputes. This ambiguity can introduce unpredictability and result in outcomes that may not align with either party's expectations. Below is an explanation of the potential complications and why specifying a governing law is essential.

What Happens Without a Governing Law Clause?

1. **Default Rules Apply**:
   In the absence of a specified governing law, the arbitration rules chosen (e.g., the American Arbitration Association (AAA) or ICC rules) often provide guidance. However, they typically defer to the "seat of arbitration" (the place where arbitration is legally based) to determine procedural matters. Substantive issues may still be unclear.

2. **Conflict of Laws**:
   Arbitrators or courts may need to conduct a "conflict of laws" analysis to determine which jurisdiction's law should apply. This can be a time-consuming and contentious process, potentially delaying the resolution of the dispute.

3. **Unintended Application of Unfavorable Laws**:
   The laws of the seat of arbitration may apply by default, even if those laws are not favorable to one or both parties. This can lead to unexpected interpretations of the contract terms or remedies.

4. **Increased Costs and Complexity**:
Disputes over which laws apply can add significant time and expense to arbitration, undermining one of the key benefits of ADR: efficiency.

Why Include a Governing Law Clause?

Specifying a governing law ensures clarity and predictability. It allows parties to:

- Know in advance which legal principles will be applied to interpret the contract and resolve disputes.
- Avoid costly and time-consuming disputes over applicable law.
- Align the law with their business interests or familiarity, especially when dealing with state or international jurisdictions.

How to Add Governing Law to an Arbitration Clause

Here's how you can revise the example clause to include a governing law provision:

> *Any dispute, controversy, or claim arising out of or relating to this contract, including the breach, termination, or validity thereof, shall be resolved by arbitration administered by [Designated Arbitration Institution] in accordance with its [specific rules]. The arbitration shall be conducted in the English language, and the place of arbitration shall be [City, State]. This contract shall be governed by and construed in accordance with the laws of [Chosen State]. The arbitral tribunal shall consist of [one/three] arbitrator(s) with experience in government contracting, appointed in accordance with the applicable rules. The decision of the arbitrator(s) shall be final and binding upon the*

parties, and judgment on the award rendered by the arbitrator(s) may be entered in any court of competent jurisdiction. Each party shall bear its own costs and expenses associated with the arbitration, except as otherwise determined by the arbitrator(s).

Notwithstanding the foregoing, either party may seek interim or injunctive relief from a court of competent jurisdiction to protect its rights or property pending the resolution of the arbitration.

By including both a governing law clause and a seat of arbitration, the parties ensure procedural and substantive clarity, reducing uncertainty and supporting an efficient arbitration process.

Companion Clauses

The Alternative Dispute Resolution Clause must work in harmony with the following Companion Clauses to produce an effective NDA:

Companion Clauses	Why It's Important
Choice of Law	Specifies the legal framework and venue for resolving disputes.
Notice of Breach	Requires the receiving party to promptly notify the disclosing party if covered information is disclosed or mishandled.
Remedies for Breach	Provides recourse if a breach occurs during the term of the NDA.

Companion Clauses	Why It's Important
Alternative Dispute Resolutions	Outlines the mechanism by which disagreements between parties will be addressed.
Liquidated Damages	Predefines the financial consequences of failing to protect the disclosing party's confidential information
Survivability	Extends confidentiality obligations beyond the termination of the agreement.

RETURN OF PROPRIETARY INFORMATION

Another important clause that is common and should be included in all Non Disclosure agreements, is a clause providing for the return of confidential information upon termination or natural expiration of the NDA.

Ideally, this clause will specify that the receiving party is required to return all of the disclosing party's information, and to provide a signed certificate stating that they have destroyed all copies of the information in their possession. Preferably, this clause addresses all types of electronic media as well as hardcopy data, and prohibits the other party from making any future copies of your information.

Depending on the nature of the information exchanged, the certification of destruction and the prohibition on making any further copies could create logistical issues for the parties and prove to be quite costly. This is due to the fact not all companies have the same policy regarding back-up and storage of their electronic media and systems. Actually, they may even employ a third party provider to execute and maintain electronic storage and automatic backup. So to require a company to certify that all copies have been destroyed and no other copies will be made, requires the firm to have a robust document classification system, advanced electronic storage and back-up systems and processes.

For this reason, many contractors consent to allow the other party to maintain 1 electronic copy of the information subject to the terms of the NDA. However, if doing so, the agreement should be clear that the requirement to protect such copy, or copies, shall be a perpetual requirement.

The person responsible for reviewing, and / or signing NDAs, must have a full understanding of all company policies and processes. The return of protected information requirement, and more specifically the destruction certification requirement, require the receiving party to have robust system in place with the ability to track, return or destroy, and to certify that you have properly done so. This types of requirements are not unreasonable, or uncommon, so if you don't have the ability to comply, you must put the systems in place immediately. Every Government Contractor must be able to accept these types of provisions or clauses. Everyone expects you to – and you should never sign an agreement when you know you cannot fully comply with all terms.

While the above big picture discussion highlights the importance of the requirement to return protected information to the originator, the real value lies in understanding how these principles play out in real world scenarios. Let's turn to some concrete examples that illustrate the impact and nuances of NDA clauses that govern the Return or Destruction of Proprietary Information.

The following clause is typical of most standard NDAs:

> ***Return of Proprietary Information***
> *Upon request of a Disclosing Party, a Receiving Party shall return or certify destruction of, within five (5) business days of receiving such request, all copies of any Proprietary Information of the Disclosing Party in the possession or control of the Receiving Party. However, the Receiving Party may keep one copy for auditing and records purposes only and such copy shall be held to the obligations in this Agreement in perpetuity.*

This is a very straight forward and simple clause and easy to comply with assuming the receiving party has policies, and proven practices in place to ensure all Proprietary Information received is marked appropriately and stored using methods that will enable the timely compliance with the timeframes identified in the request. The distinctive element of this clause is that the data must be returned at any time, based on the unilateral decision of the Disclosing Party. The term of the NDA has no impact, or effect on when the Disclosing Party may request return of his previously supplied information.

Another approach that is common is found in this sample clause:

> ***Return of Proprietary Information***
> *At the end of the Term of this Agreement, the Receiving Party will return to the Disclosing Party, retaining no copies, photographs, notes, or electronic files, all Proprietary Information including, but not limited to, reports, abstracts, lists, correspondence, information, electronic or computer files, media and/or data storage devices, and all other materials and all copies of such material, obtained by the Receiving Party during the term of this Agreement.*

Note, that this clause does not grant the Disclosing Party a right to request return of their information prior to the end of the term of the Agreement. Further, the obligation to return all information received under the agreement is placed on the Receiving Party, and it is not an optional obligation. It is a requirement that is automatically activated at the end of the Term of the agreement.

Just as before, compliance with this clauses requires the receiving party to have a proven system of tracking and storing another firms protected information. Also, the requirement to return "data storage devices" could create ambiguities and miscommunication, unless both parties have a full understanding of owns title to such "data storage devices". Typically, one would only return devices if they were provided to the receiving party by the disclosing party.

Another potential issue with this language is that the requirement that the receiving party will retain no copies. Before agreeing to this type language, it is important to fully understand your company's internal systems and processes for back-up of all servers, email and other computer systems or elements of the system.

Another scenario to consider is this version of the Clause:

> **Return of Proprietary Information**
> *The Receiving Party will, upon a written request from the Disclosing Party, return all copies and records of any Proprietary Information to the Disclosing Party and will not retain any copies or records of any Proprietary Information belonging to the Disclosing Party.*

Potential issues with a clause written in this manner, is that there is not a timeframe required, or agreed upon, for the Receiving Party to comply with Disclosing parties' direction to return the information.

How must they be returned? Clearly you cannot email them because then you create an electronic file of the information.

Also, what if you have multiple NDAs currently active – each for a separate purpose – with the same party. As written, this clause does not allow you to retain any information received under another Agreement, because the clause includes the phrase "return all copies and records of any Proprietary Information".

Most often, Clauses associated with Return or Destruction of Information may survive the duration or term of the NDA, and the receiving party promises to always protect the confidentiality of the information.

These real-world examples illustrate the complexities and trade-offs involved, when structuring a NDA for your firm, or when negotiating the terms presented to you for consideration. At the same time they also point us toward a path that balances the needs of all parties.

The best negotiated option then most likely may be something that resembles this potential clause:

> ***Return of Proprietary Information***
> *At any time during the term of this agreement, or any specified protection period, the Disclosing party may provide a written request to the Receiving Party for return or destruction of all copies of any Proprietary Information of the Disclosing Party in the possession or control of the Receiving Party that was exchanged for the specific purpose identified in this agreement. The Receiving Party agrees to provide a full, complete, and timely response to the Disclosing Parties' request within five (5) business days of receiving such request. Any time one party elects, or is required, to destroy the other parties protected information, the party performing such destruction shall send the other party a written notice of destruction which has been duly certified by an appropriate representative of the party. However, the Receiving Party may keep one copy for auditing and records purposes only and such copy shall be held to the obligations in this Agreement in perpetuity.*
>
> *If the Purpose of this Agreement includes the submission of a proposal by one of the Parties which would incorporate Proprietary Information of the other Party, then the receiving Party may retain copies of the proposal for its internal use, including*

the Proprietary Information of the disclosing Party, provided that no use may be made of the Proprietary Information other than for the stated Purpose of this Agreement. The Parties understand that copies of such proposals may be retained by customers to whom they were submitted

Companion Clauses

The Return of Proprietary Information Clause must work in harmony with the following Companion Clauses to produce an effective NDA:

Companion Clauses	Why It's Important
Term or Duration Period	Works directly with the Effective Date to define when the NDA starts and how long confidentiality obligations remain in effect.
Standards of Care	Sets clear obligations for the receiving party to protect the information shared.
Survivability	Extends confidentiality obligations beyond the termination of the agreement.
Protection Period	Defines the period of time all disclosed information must be protected beyond the term or duration of the NDA.
Notice of Breach	Requires the receiving party to promptly notify the disclosing

Companion Clauses	Why It's Important
	party if covered information is disclosed or mishandled.
Remedies for Breach	Provides recourse if a breach occurs during the term of the NDA.
Alternative Dispute Resolutions	Outlines the mechanism by which disagreements between parties will be addressed.
Liquidated Damages	Predefines the financial consequences of failing to protect the disclosing party's confidential information
Termination	Provides an exit mechanism for ending the NDA.

ASSIGNMENT

The assignment clause is one of the most frequently misunderstood provisions in Non-Disclosure Agreements (NDAs). While it may appear straightforward, disagreements over what constitutes an assignment can often lead to disputes between the parties.

Adding to the confusion, NDAs often include both Assignment and Change of Control clauses. Although related, these clauses serve different purposes, and understanding their distinctions is critical for contracting professionals. Despite their distinct purposes, the confusion among these two principal concepts often stems from the fact that both clauses deal with changes to the parties involved in an agreement. However, while an Assignment involves the transfer of rights and obligations, a Change of Control involves a shift in a party's ownership or control structure without necessarily involving an assignment.

The confusion may also arise from the fact that changes of control often trigger the application of Assignment Clauses. For example, during a merger, a Change of Control Clause may be triggered, leading to a situation where the NDA's obligations are assigned to the new entity. However, the Assignment Clause will govern how that assignment is handled and whether it is permissible.

For these reasons, it's essential to include a formal definition of assignment within the assignment clause of every non-disclosure agreement.

What is Assignment in Federal Contracting?

In a contractual context, an assignment refers to the transfer of rights or benefits under an agreement from one party to another. For federal contractors, this often relates to the right to enforce obligations, such as confidentiality, under an NDA.

For example, if a prime contractor enters a NDA with a potential subcontractor and later merges with another company, the acquiring company may need to enforce the NDA to protect sensitive information. Without a properly drafted Assignment Clause, the acquiring company might lack the legal authority to do so, exposing proprietary information to potential misuse.

Why Should Prime Contractors Be Concerned About Assignment?

Federal contractors operate in a dynamic industry where mergers, acquisitions, and restructuring are common. These events create potential vulnerabilities if NDAs lack clear assignment provisions. Here are two reasons why assignment is a concern:

Continuity in Enforcement: Without an Assignment Clause, the ability to enforce confidentiality obligations may not automatically transfer to a successor entity, leaving sensitive information unprotected.

Unauthorized Transfers: A party might assign its rights under the NDA to an entity that the other party did not agree to work with, introducing potential risks or conflicts.

Prime contractors may view an assignment by one of their subcontractors as an indication that the subcontractor is facing financial difficulties that could impact their ability to fulfill current, or future contractual obligations.

Consequently, prime contractors routinely require their approval or consent before any assignments can take place.

Subcontractors, on the other hand, may push back against these requirements. They may request that consent requirements be replaced with notification provisions. If the prime contractor is unwilling to accept this change, the subcontractor should advocate for a specific timeline for the prime to respond to assignment requests. If no response is given within the stipulated timeframe, the request should be considered approved.

What Should an Assignment Clause Allow and Prohibit?

To strike the right balance, an Assignment Clause in a prime contractor NDA should address the following:

What the Agreement Should Allow:

1. **Assignment to Affiliates or Successors:** The clause should permit assignment in specific, predictable scenarios, such as:
   - Corporate mergers or acquisitions.
   - Transfers to a wholly owned subsidiary or affiliate.
2. **Binding Successors:** Ensure that the agreement explicitly binds successors and assigns to the same obligations as the original parties.

What the Agreement Should Prohibit:

1. **Unauthorized Transfers:** Prohibit assignment without prior written consent from the other party to prevent the NDA from being assigned to unrelated or undesirable entities.
2. **Unilateral Assignment:** Prevent either party from unilaterally transferring rights under the NDA without clear parameters, as this can lead to enforcement challenges.

Potential Negotiation Nuances

Subcontractors routinely find the consent or approval requirement cumbersome and may seek to replace the prior consent language with simpler notification provisions. Their argument typically revolves around flexibility and the desire for smoother business operations, especially in large projects where changes in personnel or business structure are common. By requesting only notification, subcontractors may want to ensure that assignments can occur more fluidly without unnecessary delays or potential roadblocks from the prime contractor.

If the prime contractor remains firm on requiring consent, subcontractors should advocate for a compromise that establishes a reasonable timeline for the prime contractor's response to any assignment request. A typical negotiation strategy might involve setting a clear timeframe — such as 10 or 15 business days — for the prime to either approve or deny the proposed assignment. If the prime contractor does not respond within this window, the subcontractor could argue that the assignment should be automatically deemed approved. This approach provides some level of certainty and avoids prolonged delays that could affect the subcontractor's ability to execute the contract effectively.

Incorporating a timeline for response in assignment clauses strikes a balance between the prime contractor's desire for control and the subcontractor's need for operational flexibility. It also helps avoid the risk of bottlenecks in a project, which could hinder progress and impact deadlines. For both parties, it's essential that any such timelines are clearly defined within the NDA to ensure that expectations are aligned and that neither party is left in a position of uncertainty. In the end, open communication and a mutual understanding of each party's priorities are critical to crafting an assignment clause that is both fair and effective in the context of government contracting

Distinguishing Assignment, Novation, and Delegation in NDAs

Assignment is often misunderstood or conflated with other contract concepts, besides the Change In Control concept, such as novation and delegation. Understanding these distinctions is essential: Novation involves replacing one of the original parties with a new party, requiring the consent of all involved. The original party is released from obligations under the contract. Delegation refers to transferring obligations under a contract but does not relieve the original party of liability unless specifically agreed. In contrast, assignment in a NDA focuses solely on transferring rights, such as the right to enforce confidentiality obligations. Obligations, like maintaining the confidentiality of disclosed information, cannot be assigned without renegotiating the agreement.

Industry-Standard Assignment Clauses

Here is an example of a clause that requires consent of the other party:

> ***Assignment***
> *Neither party may assign or transfer this Agreement, or any rights or obligations hereunder, without the prior written consent of the other party, which consent shall not unreasonably be withheld. Any consent request not responded to within ten (10) calendar days shall be determined to be acceptable and agreed to by all parties.. This consent requirement shall not apply in the event either party shall change its corporate name. Any attempted assignment in violation of this provision shall be null and void. This Agreement shall be binding upon and inure to the benefit of the parties and their respective successors and permitted assigns.*

Here is an example of a clause where only a notice of assignment is required:

> ***Advance Notice of Assignment***
> *Neither party may assign or transfer its rights or obligations under this Agreement, in whole or in part, to any third party without prior written notification to the other party. Such notification shall*

be provided no less than forty-five [45] calendar days before the proposed assignment takes effect, and shall include details of the assignment, including the name of the assignee, the rights and obligations being assigned, and any relevant information necessary for the other party to assess the impact of the assignment.

If the receiving party does not object in writing within fifteen [15] calendar days following the notification, the assignment shall be deemed approved. Failure to respond within this timeframe shall be considered as acceptance of the assignment. Any attempted assignment in violation of this provision shall be null and void. This Agreement shall be binding upon and inure to the benefit of the parties and their respective successors and permitted assigns.

NDAs are foundational tools for protecting sensitive information, and they must be carefully constructed to remain enforceable in a fluid business environment. An Assignment Clause ensures that rights and obligations under the agreement are preserved, even as companies evolve through mergers, acquisitions, or reorganizations.

By including clear language that allows appropriate assignments while prohibiting unauthorized transfers, contractors can safeguard their proprietary information and maintain strong legal protections. Take the time to review and refine your NDAs to include an Assignment Clause that anticipates the realities of today's contracting landscape.

Companion Clauses

The Assignment Clause must work in harmony with the following Companion Clauses to produce an effective NDA:

Companion Clauses	Why It's Important
Change of Control or Ownership	Defines what happens to the NDA when one party experiences a change in ownership, merger, acquisition, or control
Choice of Law	Specifies the legal framework and venue for resolving disputes.
Permitted Disclosure	Allows disclosures under defined circumstances.
Notice of Breach	Requires the receiving party to promptly notify the disclosing party if covered information is disclosed or mishandled.
Remedies for Breach	Provides recourse if a breach occurs during the term of the NDA.
Termination	Provides an exit mechanism for ending the NDA.

CHANGE OF CONTROL OR OWNERSHIP

A Change of Control addresses what happens to the agreement if one of the parties undergoes a significant ownership or structural change, such as a merger, acquisition, or sale of controlling interest. Not all contractors use a Change of Control clause in their "boilerplate" agreement because they rely on their internal due diligence monitoring efforts, and other stringent clauses to protect their interests. These stringent clauses often include non-assignment provisions, confidentiality obligations, and intellectual property protections, which collectively help safeguard against risks arising from changes in the other party's structure or ownership.

However, relying solely on internal monitoring or related clauses can leave gaps in oversight. A Change of Control clause provides explicit contractual terms to ensure that any significant ownership or management changes are disclosed, enabling parties to evaluate potential risks and respond appropriately. For example, the acquiring company in a merger may have different operational practices or risk profiles that could affect the security of sensitive information or compliance with federal contracting requirements.

Including a Change of Control clause not only strengthens the agreement but also demonstrates a proactive approach to mitigating risks associated with business transitions. This can be especially critical in the government contracting arena, where compliance, confidentiality, and trust are paramount. The major benefit of include a Change of Control clause is that it safeguards against the possibility of proprietary or sensitive information being inadvertently transferred to a third party, especially one that may be a competitor or otherwise undesirable partner.

Clauses Intertwined with "Change of Control" Provisions

Several clauses are often closely linked to Change of Control provisions:

1. **Assignment Clauses:** A Change of Control event may involve implicit assignment of rights and obligations under the NDA, so the two clauses must align.

2. **Confidentiality Obligations:** The clause must ensure that confidentiality commitments survive the Change of Control and bind any successor entity.

3. **Termination Clauses:** The other party may want the right to terminate the NDA if the Change of Control involves a transfer to a direct competitor or adversarial party.

4. **Notification Requirements:** Parties typically require notification of a Change of Control within a specified timeframe, ensuring transparency.

Understanding Change of Control Notification in NDAs

Change of Control provisions address shifts in a company's ownership or management structure, such as mergers, acquisitions, or changes in majority ownership.

It is entirely reasonable for both parties to want to know if a member of their contractual team is about to experience changes in a company's ownership or management structure, such as mergers, acquisitions, or changes in majority ownership. Including a Notification Requirement in such provisions ensures transparency and allows the other party to evaluate the implications of the change on their interests and the security of shared information.

However, it's important to understand what notification entails. Notification simply means that one party is required to inform the other about a Change of Control—it does not grant the receiving party the authority to approve or reject the change. In essence, notification is a courtesy and a transparency measure, not a veto power.

Timing of Notifications: Practical Challenges

In some cases, you may negotiate for "advance notification," requiring the party undergoing the change to inform the other party about the impending event before it occurs—typically 30 days in advance. While this is ideal in theory, it is often not feasible in practice.

For instance, in the case of mergers or acquisitions, the party experiencing the Change of Control may be legally or contractually restricted from disclosing such information before the deal is finalized. In these situations, notifications may only be possible after the event has occurred. It's important for contractors to remain flexible and realistic when negotiating the timing of such notifications.

Example Clause

Here is a sample Change of Control Clause that is common for inclusion into NDAs:

> ***Change of Control***
> *In the event of a Change of Control of either party, the party experiencing the Change of Control ("Affected Party") shall promptly notify the other party in writing no later than [X] calendar days after the Change of Control occurs. For the purposes of this Agreement, "Change of Control" shall mean a transaction or series of transactions resulting in:*
>
> *a) the sale, transfer, or assignment of more than fifty percent (50%) of the Affected Party's ownership interests.*
> *b) the merger, consolidation, or reorganization of the Affected Party with another entity that results in a change in the party's controlling interest; or*

c) the sale, transfer, or assignment of all or substantially all of the Affected Party's assets.

Upon receipt of notice of a Change of Control, the other party may, at its sole discretion:

1. Terminate this Agreement with [X] calendar days' written notice if the Change of Control involves a transfer to a competitor or entity adverse to the terminating party's interests; or
2. Require the Affected Party or its successor entity to reaffirm in writing its obligations under this Agreement within [X] business days of notice.

The confidentiality and non-use obligations of this Agreement shall survive any Change of Control and bind any successor or assign of the Affected Party.

This provision incorporates two key elements that may be contentious during negotiations: (1) the requirement to "shall promptly notify," and (2) the specified timeline of "[X] days after the Change of Control occurs."

In many cases, the other party may prefer notification requirements to mandate advance notice rather than notification after the event. They want to be informed before the change occurs, allowing them to assess and address potential risks proactively. To accommodate this preference, companies often attempt to revise the clause to require advance notification, such that the final clause would read:

Change of Control
In the event of a Change of Control of either party, the party experiencing the Change of Control ("Affected Party") shall provide an advance written notification to the other party, no less than forty-five [45] calendar days before the Change of Control

occurs. For the purposes of this Agreement, "Change of Control" shall mean a transaction or series of transactions resulting in:

a) the sale, transfer, or assignment of more than fifty percent (50%) of the Affected Party's ownership interests.
b) the merger, consolidation, or reorganization of the Affected Party with another entity that results in a change in the party's controlling interest; or
c) the sale, transfer, or assignment of all or substantially all of the Affected Party's assets.

Upon receipt of notice of a Change of Control, the other party may, at its sole discretion:

1. Terminate this Agreement with [X] calendar days' written notice if the Change of Control involves a transfer to a competitor or entity adverse to the terminating party's interests; or
2. Require the Affected Party or its successor entity to reaffirm in writing its obligations under this Agreement within [X] business days of notice.

The confidentiality and non-use obligations of this Agreement shall survive any Change of Control and bind any successor or assign of the Affected Party.

Requiring advance notification of a Change of Control provides parties with the opportunity to assess potential risks and make informed decisions before the event occurs, safeguarding their interests and the integrity of the agreement. This proactive approach ensures transparency and allows for necessary adjustments, such as reevaluating confidentiality obligations or terminating the agreement if the new ownership poses a conflict of interest. Conversely, receiving notification only after the change has occurred may leave parties exposed to unforeseen operational and legal risks without adequate time to respond.

Why This Clause Is Considered Acceptable:

- **Transparency:** It mandates advance notification of a potential issue, ensuring the other party is aware of ownership changes.
- **Flexibility**: It gives the unaffected party options, such as termination or reaffirmation, in response to the Change of Control.
- **Protection:** Confidentiality obligations survive the Change of Control, ensuring sensitive information remains secure regardless of ownership changes.
- **Balance:** The clause protects both parties without unduly restricting business activities or opportunities.

While advance notifications are always the most ideal, the realities of business transactions often necessitate flexibility. A well-drafted Change of Control provision balances the need for disclosure with the practical limitations of the parties involved, ensuring that both sides are informed without imposing unreasonable burdens.

Companion Clauses

The Change of Control or Ownership Clause must work in harmony with the following Companion Clauses to produce an effective NDA:

Companion Clauses	Why It's Important
Change of Control or Ownership	Defines what happens to the NDA when one party experiences a change in ownership, merger, acquisition, or control

Companion Clauses	Why It's Important
Assignment	Prevents parties from transferring their obligations under the NDA to third parties without consent.
Notice of Breach	Requires the receiving party to promptly notify the disclosing party if covered information is disclosed or mishandled.
Standards of Care	Sets clear obligations for the receiving party to protect the information shared.
Responsible Parties	Identifies individuals within the named parties who are authorized to disclose or receive information
Return of Proprietary Information	Ensures confidential information is returned or destroyed when the NDA ends.
Remedies for Breach	Provides recourse if a breach occurs during the term of the NDA.
Termination	Provides an exit mechanism for ending the NDA.

IMPORT & EXPORT RESTRICTIONS

This clause not only ensures that all parties adhere to stringent U.S. export control regulations, such as the International Traffic in Arms Regulations (ITAR) and the Export Administration Regulations (EAR), but also provides clear guidelines for handling technical data that could have national security implications.

Benefits of an Import and Export Regulations Clause

The benefits of incorporating an Import and Export Regulations Clause are significant. First, the clause ensures compliance with U.S. import and export laws, reducing the risk of severe penalties such as fines, sanctions, or debarment from federal contracts. For government contractors handling sensitive information, this clause provides a robust safeguard against unintentional disclosures to unauthorized parties or foreign nationals. Additionally, it helps clarify each party's responsibilities, ensuring that the receiving party understands their obligations to handle technical data appropriately. Furthermore, the clause minimizes the potential for legal disputes and liabilities by delineating clear boundaries and offering protections to the disclosing party. Lastly, it enhances trust between the contracting parties by demonstrating a shared commitment to safeguarding sensitive information and adhering to legal obligations.

What the Clause Should Address

An effective Import and Export Regulations Clause should:

1. **Define the Applicability of U.S. Laws**
   Clearly state that ITAR and EAR regulations govern the handling of all technical data shared under the NDA.

2. **Set Clear Prohibitions**
   Prohibit the disclosure of technical data to any foreign national, firm, or country without explicit authorization.

3. **Establish Licensing Requirements**
   Mandate that the receiving party obtains necessary export licenses and secures the written consent of the disclosing party before submitting requests for export authority.

4. **Include Indemnification Terms**
   Hold the receiving party responsible for any damages, fines, or penalties resulting from non-compliance with export regulations.

5. **Provide for Administrative Oversight**
   Require both parties to maintain systems to monitor compliance, such as tracking data disclosures and employee access.

Here is a suggested clause for consideration

> *Export Regulations:*
>
> *This Agreement does not authorize export of technical data. The Receiving Party represents and warrants that no technical data furnished to it by the Disclosing Party shall be disclosed to any foreign national, nation, firm, or country, including foreign nationals employed by or associated with the Receiving Party, nor shall any technical data be exported from the United States without first complying with all U.S. export control regulations including the requirements of the International Traffic in Arms Regulations (ITAR) or the Export Administration Regulations (EAR), including the requirement for obtaining any export license if applicable. The Receiving Party shall first obtain the written consent of the Disclosing Party prior to submitting any request for authority to export any such technical data. The Receiving Party shall indemnify and hold the Disclosing Party harmless for all claims, demands, damages, costs, fines,*

penalties, attorney's fees, and all other expenses arising from failure of the Receiving Party to comply with this clause or the ITAR and EAR.

Including an Import and Export Regulations Clause in NDAs is more than a legal formality—it is a strategic necessity for government contractors. By prioritizing this provision, contractors can safeguard sensitive data, reduce risks, and demonstrate their commitment to compliance and national security.

Companion Clauses

The Import and Export Restrictions Clause must work in harmony with the following Companion Clauses to produce an effective NDA:

Companion Clauses	Why It's Important
Specific Purpose	Specifies for what purposes the Confidential / Proprietary Information can and cannot be used.
Choice of Law	Specifies the legal framework and venue for resolving disputes.
Warranties	May include assurances that the data shared is owned by the disclosing party and that no third-party rights are being violated.
Standards of Care	Sets clear obligations for the receiving party to protect the information shared.
Notice of Breach	Requires the receiving party to promptly notify the disclosing

Companion Clauses	Why It's Important
	party if covered information is disclosed or mishandled.
Restricted Use	Limits the scope of use to ensure export compliance.
Termination	Provides an exit mechanism for ending the NDA.

TERMINATION

You might ask yourself if the Termination Clause is necessary for a Non-Disclosure Agreement? In short, yes—termination clauses are essential for Non-Disclosure Agreements (NDAs). These clauses often get overlooked in favor of more high-profile contract terms, but they play a vital role in defining how the agreement may end and what obligations continue after termination. In fact, confidentiality obligations should always persist beyond the formal termination of an NDA. This ensures that proprietary information remains safeguarded even after the business relationship has concluded. Without this ongoing protection, sensitive data could become vulnerable, defeating the purpose of the NDA.

It's important to distinguish termination clauses from exit clauses (sometimes referred to as escape clauses). An exit clause provides a mechanism for one party to abandon the agreement altogether, often without fulfilling all its terms. Termination clauses, by contrast, do not allow parties to arbitrarily walk away from their obligations. Instead, they establish the terms under which a NDA can be ended while ensuring that confidentiality responsibilities persist as appropriate.

The Importance of Termination Clauses

Business relationships, like personal ones, can end unexpectedly, and this holds true even in federal contracting, where NDAs are often critical for protecting sensitive information. A well-crafted termination clause provides clarity and structure for ending the agreement, outlining the process, notice requirements, and ongoing obligations. This helps prevent disputes and potential legal issues that could arise without a clear roadmap for termination.

For instance, if one party decides the relationship is no longer beneficial or finds the other party unsuitable as a partner, the termination clause dictates how the NDA can be dissolved. Without a termination clause, disputes over timing, notice, and ongoing obligations can create uncertainty and potential legal exposure.

A Practical Safeguard

Termination clauses also ensure that parties cannot simply abandon their responsibilities under the guise of ending the agreement. Confidentiality obligations, for example, often extend well beyond the formal termination of an NDA. These clauses specify the procedures for notification, the required notice period, and the steps for returning or securely disposing of proprietary information.

In federal contracting, where sensitive data often changes hands, termination clauses are not just practical, they are essential. They protect the integrity of the information shared while offering both parties a clear roadmap for winding down the relationship.

Essentials of a Termination Clause

An effective termination clause will clearly address the following:

1. **Notice Requirements:**
   Specify how the intent to terminate must be communicated (e.g., written notice) and whether a notice period is required before termination takes effect.

2. **Post-Termination Confidentiality Obligations:**
   Define whether and how obligations of confidentiality continue after termination, ensuring that sensitive information remains protected even if the agreement ends prematurely.

For unilateral NDAs (where only one party discloses information), termination is often straightforward, particularly if the disclosing party initiates the termination. In such cases, the agreement's purpose—to protect the discloser's information—should always remain intact even after termination.

For the receiving party, however, confidentiality obligations usually survive termination for the duration specified in the agreement. Here's an example of a unilateral NDA termination clause:

> ***Sample Clause (Unilateral NDA):***
> *This agreement shall terminate three (3) years after the effective date or may be terminated by either party, for any reason, at any time by providing a thirty (30) calendar days written notice to the other party. However, the Recipient's obligation under this agreement shall survive any termination and shall bind the Recipient's heirs, successors, and assigns. Upon termination, the Recipient shall promptly return all documents and tangible materials representing the Discloser's confidential information to the "Notices" POC identified elsewhere in this agreement.*

Termination in Mutual NDAs

Mutual NDAs, where both parties disclose sensitive information, add complexity. Both parties typically remain bound by confidentiality obligations even after termination, as stipulated in the agreement. These obligations ensure fairness and protect both parties' proprietary information for an agreed period post-termination.

Here's an example of a mutual NDA clause with post-termination confidentiality obligations:

> ***Sample Termination Clause (Mutual NDA):***
> *This agreement shall expire three (3) years after the effective date or may be terminated by either party*

> *by providing the other party with a thirty (30) calendar days written notice. However, the Recipient's obligations under this agreement shall survive termination for five (5) years from the date of termination and shall bind the Recipient's heirs, successors, and assigns. Upon termination, the Recipient shall promptly return all documents and tangible materials representing the Disclosing Party's confidential information to the "Notices" POC identified elsewhere in this agreement.*

Here's an example of a stand-alone mutual termination clause that can be used when the agreement includes a definitive protection period and survivability requirements:

> **Termination:**
> *Either party may elect to terminate this agreement, at any time and for any reason, by providing the other party thirty (30) calendar days written Notice of Termination. However, the termination of this Agreement shall not relieve either party of their obligations hereunder regarding the protection and use of proprietary information disclosed hereunder prior to that date. Termination of this agreement does not alter in any way, the receiving party's obligations as addressed in the survivability requirements addressed elsewhere in this agreement. Upon termination, the Recipient shall promptly return all documents and tangible materials representing the Disclosing Party's confidential information to the POC identified elsewhere in this agreement.*

Best Practices for Contractors

For contracting professionals, it's crucial to ensure termination clauses are tailored to the nature of the relationship and the sensitivity of the shared information. Important considerations include:

- **Ensuring Clarity:** Clearly define the process for termination and post-termination responsibilities to avoid disputes.

- **Maintaining Balance:** For mutual NDAs, ensure obligations are reciprocal and equitable.

- **Protecting Interests:** Post-termination confidentiality periods should be reasonable and aligned with the nature of the information disclosed.

By thoughtfully negotiating termination provisions, contractors can protect sensitive information and foster trust, even if the business relationship comes to an early conclusion.

Companion Clauses

The Termination Clause must work in harmony with the following Companion Clauses to produce an effective NDA:

Companion Clauses	Why It's Important
Survivability	Extends confidentiality obligations beyond the termination of the agreement.
Choice of Law	Specifies the legal framework and venue for resolving disputes.
Responsible Parties	Identifies individuals within the named parties who are authorized to disclose or receive information

Companion Clauses	Why It's Important
Return of Proprietary Information	Ensures confidential information is returned or destroyed when the NDA ends.
Remedies for Breach	Provides recourse if a breach occurs during the term of the NDA.
Standards of Care	Sets clear obligations for the receiving party to protect the information shared.
Specific Purpose	Specifies for what purposes the Confidential / Proprietary Information can and cannot be used.

WARRANTIES

The Warranty Clause should address what, if anything, is warranted by the parties regarding the information disclosed under the agreement. While most contracting professionals focus on confidentiality obligations, the Warranty Clause is an equally critical component that can significantly impact risk management and liability. For both parties to the agreement, his clause must ensure that information is disclosed on clear terms, protecting the disclosing party from unintended obligations or liabilities.

Why Are Warranties a Concern for NDAs?

Including warranties—intentionally or unintentionally—can create significant risks:

1. **Risk of Liability:** If the disclosing party implicitly warrants the accuracy, completeness, or reliability of the information, they could be held liable for damages from any issues arising from the receiving party's reliance on that information.

2. **Unintended Obligations:** Without clear limitations and disclaimers, courts may infer warranties even if they were never explicitly stated. For instance, if the receiving party uses the data and suffers a loss due to errors, the disclosing party could be held responsible, even if the disclosing party has no control over how the data was used.

3. **Ambiguity and Disputes:** Ambiguous language around the quality or completeness of information can lead to disagreements and potential litigation. Courts may infer warranties or representations from the context of the agreement, exposing the disclosing party to risks they never intended to assume.

To mitigate these concerns, and avoid these pitfalls, it's crucial to include specific provisions that shield the disclosing party from any related liability and clearly define the lack of any warranty.

What Should Be Warrantied—or Not Warrantied?

In the context of NDAs, warranties are assurances regarding the quality, accuracy, or suitability of the information being disclosed. However, when disclosing sensitive information, you want to avoid providing any warranties, whether express or implied.

The language contained with the clause should explicitly state that the disclosing party makes all disclosures under these circumstances:

- The information is provided without any warranty regarding its adequacy, sufficiency, or freedom from defects.
- The disclosing party assumes no liability for how the receiving party uses the data.
- The information is provided strictly "AS IS", ensuring no implied guarantees about its accuracy, completeness, or suitability for a particular purpose.

Failing to include these disclaimers can leave the disclosing party exposed to claims if the information is found to be incomplete, incorrect, outdated, or unsuitable for the receiving party's intended use.

What the Warranty Clause Should Allow and Prohibit

A well-crafted Warranty Clause in a NDA should:

1. **Allow:**
   - **Clear Disclaimer of Warranties:** Clearly state that the information is provided "AS IS," without any warranties, whether express or implied. This removes any implied

obligations regarding the accuracy, completeness, or usability of the information.
- **Limitation of Liability:** Explicitly release the disclosing party from any liability for the use, interpretation, or outcomes related to the disclosed information. The clause should make clear that the disclosing party is not responsible for the consequences of the receiving party's decisions based on the information.

2. **Prohibit:**
   - **Implied Guarantees:** Avoid language that could inadvertently suggest the information is accurate, complete, or fit for any particular purpose.
   - **Ongoing Obligations:** Do not commit to updating or correcting previously disclosed information. Always, steer clear of provisions requiring the disclosing party to update or correct the information after disclosure unless explicitly required because of a specific purpose and the appropriate language has been negotiated into the agreement.

Example of an Industry Standard Warranty Clause

Here's an example of a Warranty Clause suitable for federal contracting NDAs:

> ***Warranty Disclaimer:***
> *The Disclosing Party makes no representations or warranties, express or implied, as to the accuracy, completeness, adequacy, sufficiency, or freedom from defect of any kind, including freedom from any patent infringement that may result from the use of such Proprietary Information provided under this Agreement. All information is provided "AS IS" and without any warranties of merchantability or fitness for a particular purpose. Neither Party shall incur any liability or obligation whatsoever by reason of*

such information. The Receiving Party acknowledges that the Disclosing Party shall have no liability arising from the use, reliance, or interpretation of the Proprietary Information by the Receiving Party or any third party.

Practical Considerations When Negotiating Clause Content

1. **Tailor the Clause to the Context:** Ensure the language of the Warranty Clause aligns with the nature of the information being disclosed and the specific goals of the NDA.

2. **Avoid Express or Implied Warranties:** Never promise or suggest that the information disclosed is free from defects or suitable for the receiving party's desired use. Use explicit disclaimers to protect against inferred obligations.

3. **Limit Liability:** Ensure the NDA explicitly absolves the disclosing party from all liability for any consequences arising from the receiving party's use of the disclosed data.

4. **Include an "AS IS" Provision:** Providing information on an "AS IS" basis makes it clear that the disclosing party is not responsible for the quality or usability of the data.

5. **Avoid Overpromising:** Even subtle language implying that the disclosed information is complete or accurate can create unintended liabilities. Be precise and clear in all descriptions of the information

Warranty Clauses protect the disclosing party by ensuring that no unintended guarantees or liabilities arise from the disclosure of sensitive information. A well-crafted Warranty Clause can be the difference between a secure partnership and an expensive legal dispute.

By including explicit disclaimers, limiting liability, and providing information "AS IS," contractors can safeguard their interests and reduce the risk of disputes. Whether drafting or reviewing an NDA, federal contracting professionals should treat the Warranty Clause as a critical element, ensuring that it aligns with the organization's risk management strategy and contractual goals.

Companion Clauses

The Warranties Clause must work in harmony with the following Companion Clauses to produce an effective NDA:

Companion Clauses	**Why It's Important**
Remedies for Breach	Provides recourse if a breach occurs during the term of the NDA.
Standards of Care	Sets clear obligations for the receiving party to protect the information shared.
Notice of Breach	Requires the receiving party to promptly notify the disclosing party if covered information is disclosed or mishandled.
Termination	Provides an exit mechanism if warranties are breached
Alternative Dispute Resolutions	Outlines the mechanism by which disagreements between parties will be addressed.
Liquidated Damages	Predefines the financial consequences of failing to protect

Companion Clauses	Why It's Important
	the disclosing party's confidential information

LIQUIDATED DAMAGES

A Liquidated Damages Clause establishes a predetermined amount of damages that the breaching party must pay in the event of a confidentiality breach. This provides several key benefits:

- **Deterrence:** The threat of significant financial liability can powerfully deter subcontractors from disclosing confidential information.

- **Simplified Enforcement:** Without a Liquidated Damages Clause, contractors may need to engage in costly and time-consuming litigation to prove the actual damages resulting from a breach. With such a clause in place, the damages are already clearly defined and the parties have established a clear and enforceable remedy upfront.

- **Predictable Risk Management:** By establishing a known potential liability, all parties to the agreement know the financial consequences of a breach which encourages better risk management and planning.

- **Clarity and Predictability:** By pre-determining the consequences of a breach, both parties are able to avoid protracted disputes over the extent of damages in the event of a violation. This ensures smoother enforcement of the NDA terms and avoids the far-reaching consequences of extended delays.

Key Considerations and Potential Risks

Contractors should also be cautious with liquidated damages clauses. If the pre-determined damages amount is deemed excessive or unreasonable, it may be viewed as punitive rather than compensatory. Courts are often reluctant to enforce such clauses, particularly if the amount is disproportionate to the actual harm caused and the damages seem more like a punishment than a fair estimate of harm.

Additionally, a clause that imposes liquidated damages for unintentional disclosures—such as those that occur despite reasonable efforts to protect the information—could unfairly penalize a party acting in good faith.

Furthermore, any ambiguity in the language of the agreement, is likely to create disputes over whether the receiving party met the standard of "Reasonable Care" in protecting confidential information, complicating the enforcement of any liquidated damages clauses.

Disputes can also arise over whether the standard of "reasonable care" to measure a party's responsibility was met, complicating enforcement of the clause.

Best Practices for Drafting a Clause

When drafting or negotiating a Liquidated Damages Clause, the following considerations are key:

- **Reasonable Damage Amounts:** It should reflect the potential harm that could be caused by a breach but not be so excessive that it could be seen as punitive.

- **Clear Definitions of a Breach:** Specify that liquidated damages apply to material breaches, such as intentional or grossly negligent disclosures. Exclude inadvertent or accidental breaches where the receiving party demonstrates reasonable care in protecting the information.

- **Defined Procedures for Claims:** Establish clear procedures for claiming liquidated damages, including timelines for notification and requirements for substantiating the claim.

Example of a Balanced Liquidated Damages Clause

Here is an example of a balanced liquidated damages clause for NDAs:

> **Liquidated Damages**
> *The parties agree that in the event of a material breach of this Agreement by the Receiving Party, the Disclosing Party shall be entitled to liquidated damages in the amount of $[X], representing a reasonable estimate of the potential harm caused by such a breach. This provision shall not apply to inadvertent or accidental disclosures if the Receiving Party demonstrates that it exercised the same degree of care to protect the Disclosing Party's Proprietary Information as it uses to protect its own confidential information.*

This language provides a fair and enforceable approach, limiting the application of liquidated damages to intentional or grossly negligent breaches while protecting against undue penalties for accidental disclosures.

When Liquidated Damages May Not Be Appropriate

Despite their potential benefits, liquidated damages clauses are not always appropriate for NDAs. The harm caused by breaches of confidentiality is often challenging to quantify, and the inclusion of such a clause may overcomplicate the agreement. Many professionals advocate for removing liquidated damages clauses from NDAs altogether, instead relying on traditional legal remedies or indemnification provisions to address breaches.

Striking the Right Balance

Liquidated damages clauses can be a powerful tool in NDAs for government contractors, offering clarity, deterrence, and efficiency in resolving breaches. However, they can also introduce unfair penalties and unintended liabilities if not carefully drafted.

For contracting professionals, the goal is to craft a clause that balances deterrence with fairness. By limiting the application of liquidated damages to intentional violations and excluding inadvertent errors, contractors can create agreements that protect sensitive information while maintaining enforceability and mutual trust. Whether you include a liquidated damages provision or opt to exclude it, the ultimate goal should be to protect sensitive information while ensuring fairness and enforceability in the agreement.

Companion Clauses

The Liquidated Damages Clause must work in harmony with the following Companion Clauses to produce an effective NDA:

Companion Clauses	**Why It's Important**
Notice of Breach	Requires the receiving party to promptly notify the disclosing party if covered information is disclosed or mishandled.
Remedies for Breach	Provides recourse if a breach occurs during the term of the NDA.
Alternative Dispute Resolutions	Outlines the mechanism by which disagreements between parties will be addressed.
Return of Proprietary Information	Ensures confidential information is returned or destroyed when the NDA ends.

Companion Clauses	Why It's Important
Survivability	Extends confidentiality obligations beyond the termination of the agreement.

RESPONSIBLE PARTIES

This clause specifies the individuals responsible for the administration of the NDA, ensuring clear communication, accountability, and effective management throughout the agreement's lifecycle.

Why Identification of Responsible Parties Matter

At its core, the Responsible Parties Clause designates a **Point of Contact (POC)** for each party. These individuals are responsible for receiving all proprietary information, submitting and managing notices, and ensuring compliance with various other provisions of the NDA.

One key reason this clause is critical is that NDAs SHOULD cover only **written and marked information**, meaning that ensuring the proper receipt and acknowledgment of such information by the designated POC is essential for the agreement to be enforceable. Without a named POC, there can be confusion about where sensitive information should be sent, potentially exposing contractors to risks of non-compliance or breaches.

Additionally, the POC plays a central role in executing and managing key clauses within the NDA. Notices for actions such as modifications, terminations, cancellations, disputes, import/export compliance, and liability matters must be submitted to the designated POC. This ensures that all communications are routed through the proper channels, providing a clear record and reducing the likelihood of disputes arising from misunderstandings or administrative oversights.

Another critical reason for identifying administrators is that changing the POCs requires a **bilateral agreement and signatures from both parties**. This stipulation ensures continuity and prevents unauthorized alterations to the agreement's management structure, safeguarding the integrity of the NDA.

Benefits for Contractors

For contractors, an Administrator Identification Clause delivers several benefits. First, it provides clarity and structure. By designating specific individuals, the parties eliminate ambiguity about who is responsible for receiving information and managing notices. This clarity is particularly valuable in complex government contracts where multiple agreements may be in place simultaneously.

Second, the clause enhances compliance and enforceability. When specific administrators are named, the parties can demonstrate adherence to the NDA's procedural requirements, which is critical if disputes arise. Additionally, having clear points of contact streamlines communication, ensuring that sensitive information is handled efficiently and securely.

Finally, the clause helps contractors manage risk. In situations involving disputes, liability issues, or regulatory compliance, having a designated POC simplifies the process of determining responsibility and ensures that critical communications are documented and traceable.

The following clause is offered as a reference example:

> ***Responsible Parties***
> *In order for either party's Proprietary Information to be protected as described herein, it must be appropriately marked and submitted in written form as or if disclosures will include oral discloses or visually demonstrations (for example, software), a written summary of such disclosures that reasonably identifies the proprietary information, and the*

marked written summary must be submitted to the following exclusive points of contact:

Party 1	*Party 2*
Company Name	*Company Name*
Name:	*Name:*
Title:	*Title:*
Address:	*Address:*
City, State, Zip:	*City, State, Zip:*
Phone:	*Phone:*
E-mail:	*E-mail:*

The above designated POCs are responsible for receiving all marked written declarations of protection, storing and safeguarding the information received, and managing compliance with all other provisions of this agreement.

Either party may change this point of contact by providing written notice to the other party. Delegation of responsibilities to any other individual without prior approval from both parties is strictly prohibited.

Best Practices

To maximize the effectiveness of an Administrator Identification Clause, contractors should ensure that the named POCs are properly trained and aware of their responsibilities. Regular updates to contact information should be communicated promptly, and any changes to the POCs should follow the formal process outlined in the agreement. Additionally, contractors should integrate this clause with their broader contract management systems to ensure seamless handling of NDA-related obligations.

By designating specific individuals responsible for administration, contractors can enhance communication, streamline compliance, and mitigate risks. For government contractors, this clause is an essential element of a robust NDA.

Companion Clauses

The Responsible Parties Clause must work in harmony with the following Companion Clauses to produce an effective NDA:

Companion Clauses	**Why It's Important**
Affiliates and Third Parties	Extends confidentiality obligations to affiliates, subsidiaries, representatives, subcontractors, or other third-party agents of the receiving party
Notice of Breach	Requires the receiving party to promptly notify the disclosing party if covered information is disclosed or mishandled
Permitted Disclosure	Allows disclosures under defined circumstances.
Return of Proprietary Information	Ensures confidential information is returned or destroyed when the NDA ends.

Companion Clauses	Why It's Important
Remedies for Breach	Provides recourse if a breach occurs during the term of the NDA.
Termination	Provides an exit mechanism for ending the NDA.

SEVERABLE

Severability clauses are not always standard in NDAs, their inclusion offers distinct advantages that can safeguard the integrity of the agreement. This provision ensures that if one part of the NDA is found invalid or unenforceable, the remainder of the agreement remains intact. While severability clauses are more commonly associated with Teaming Agreements, their utility in NDAs should not be overlooked.

What is a Severability Clause?

A severability clause informs courts that the agreement as a whole should not be invalidated if one provision is found unenforceable. Without a severability clause, a judge or jury may void the entire contract due to a single flawed provision. By including this clause, the enforceable parts of the NDA remain binding, ensuring that the agreement's overarching purpose is preserved.

Purpose and Benefits of a Severability Clause

The primary purpose of a severability clause is to preserve the enforceability of the remaining provisions of a contract. In NDAs, this ensures that the agreement continues to protect sensitive and proprietary information, even if a specific clause is invalidated.

Why Severability Clauses Are Important for Government Contractors:

1. **Compliance with Federal and State Laws:**
   NDAs for government contractors often operate across multiple jurisdictions, each with unique legal standards. A severability clause protects the agreement's enforceability even if a provision conflicts with local or federal law.

2. **Preservation of Intent:**

The fundamental purpose of a NDA is to safeguard sensitive information. A severability clause ensures that minor invalid provisions don't undermine the agreement's overall intent.

3. **Mitigation of Legal Risks:**
   Without a severability clause, a single flawed provision could invalidate the entire NDA, leaving contractors vulnerable. Including this clause reduces the risk of losing critical protections due to technicalities or legal challenges.

4. **Support for Related Provisions:**
   Severability clauses reinforce the intent and applicability of other standard NDA provisions, such as governing law, liability, termination, and survivability clauses.

When to Use Severability Clauses in NDAs

Severability clauses are particularly valuable in complex NDAs or agreements that involve regulatory or multi-jurisdictional concerns. For example, clauses addressing liability, intellectual property, or non-compete restrictions may be subject to differing interpretations or legal challenges in certain jurisdictions. A severability clause ensures that the rest of the agreement remains enforceable if one of these provisions is struck down.

What Should a Severability Clause Address?

A well-drafted severability clause should:

1. **Preserve the Valid Portions of the Agreement:**
   Clearly state that if a provision is found invalid or unenforceable, the remaining provisions will remain binding, and avoid vague language that might allow key provisions—

such as confidentiality obligations—to be challenged or excluded.

2. **Allow for Modification:**
   Include language permitting the adjustment of invalid provisions to align with legal standards, ensuring enforceability.

3. **Avoid Ambiguity:**
   Ensure the clause is specific enough to apply to provisions that are severed while maintaining the agreement's original intent. Exercise care so not to create any direct or indirect ambiguity that could lead to disputes over how the remaining agreement is applied.

Example of Severability Clauses

> *Severability:*
> *If any provision, provision title, or the application of any aspect thereof, or any portion of this Agreement are held to be unenforceable, illegal, or void by a court of competent jurisdiction, for any reason whatsoever, the remaining provisions hereof shall nevertheless remain enforceable, and the court making such determination shall modify the provisions hereof held to be unenforceable so as to preserve the enforceability of this Agreement to the maximum extent permitted by applicable law. The failure of either party to enforce any provision contained herein shall not be deemed a waiver of any other provision contained herein*

While severability clauses may not always be standard in NDAs, their inclusion offers significant benefits because they ensure that the agreement remains enforceable even if a single provision is invalidated, preserving the intent of the NDA and protecting sensitive information.

Companion Clauses

The Severable Clause must work in harmony with the following Companion Clauses to produce an effective NDA:

Companion Clauses	Why It's Important
Survivability	Extends confidentiality obligations beyond the termination of the agreement.
Choice of Law	Specifies the legal framework and venue for resolving disputes.
Remedies for Breach	Provides recourse if a breach occurs during the term of the NDA.
Entire Agreement	Ensures that external or prior agreements are not subject to conflicting laws or interpretations
Termination	Provides an exit mechanism for ending the NDA.

SURVIVABLE TERMS

A survival clause will determine which parts of the NDA remain enforceable after the agreement itself has ended. These clauses are essential for protecting a party's rights and obligations even after the initial agreement has been fulfilled or terminated.

However, when it comes to survival clauses in NDAs, things aren't always as straightforward as they seem. You might expect a neatly packaged clause clearly outlining what survives termination. But that's not always the case. Sometimes, the requirement for survival is cleverly hidden within the language of individual clauses themselves. There might not be a single, obvious "survival clause" to point to. This means that anyone expecting to understand what terms will outlast the NDA's expiration needs to do their due diligence. A thorough, clause-by-clause analysis of the entire document is essential. Without it, you risk missing critical details about what's intended to survive. It's a reminder that in the world of government contracting, the devil is often in the details. Don't just assume survival clauses will be easy to spot. Be prepared to roll up your sleeves and really dig into that NDA.

Survival Clauses in Non-Disclosure Agreements (NDAs)

The designation of clauses that survive the fulfillment or termination of an agreement are particularly important when sensitive information is shared during any type of business negotiations or proposal development. After all, some privileged information, such as trade secrets or patents, must remain confidential for the sake of a company's continued survival.

Types of Survival Clauses in NDAs

Survival clauses in NDAs can take various forms, each suited to different circumstances and levels of complexity. From general survival terms to those tied to specific sections, embedded within provisions, or defined by time periods or indefinite durations, each type serves a unique purpose. A prudent contracting professional must understand the roles and applications of each type of clause in order to negotiate terms that are favorable to any particular situation.

General Survival Clauses:

In some Non-Disclosure Agreements (NDAs), survival clauses are written in general terms, using language such as: *"All provisions that logically should survive the termination of this agreement will remain in effect."* This approach relies on common law standards to determine which terms persist after the NDA ends.

For straightforward business relationships and uncomplicated agreements, this general approach may be sufficient. It provides flexibility and avoids over-complicating the agreement for scenarios where the scope of privileged information is clear and the relationship between the parties is solid.

However, for more complex arrangements — such as those involving sensitive government contracts, layered partnerships, or long-term obligations — a generic survival clause might not offer enough precision or protection.

Section Number Survival Clauses

By explicitly outlining which terms survive, precise survival clauses provide clarity for both parties, reduce ambiguity, and help prevent disputes. In agreements involving intricate business relationships, this approach ensures that critical protections remain enforceable without leaving room for interpretation.

Section Number survival clauses typically reference specific sections by number or clearly identify the terms that will survive, such as confidentiality obligations or return of proprietary information.

This level of precision is particularly useful for lengthy or complex NDAs where some provisions need to extend beyond the termination of the contract while others naturally expire with it.

Here is an example of a Section Number Survival clause:

> ***Survival***
> *Unless otherwise stated within this document, the provisions set forth in Articles 2, 3.5, 3.6, 3.7, 6, 8 9.1, 13.1, 13.2, 13.6, 13.7, 18 and 21, and any related remedies shall survive the termination, or natural expiration of the term of this agreement for an additional five (5) years.*

Embedded Survival Provisions

NDAs can also be written to include survival terms directly within specific provisions, separate from any other survival clause. However, this approach can introduce ambiguity if the language isn't clear, so careful wording is essential. For instance, a sentence similar to the below example may be contained in any individual provision.

> *Notwithstanding the requirement of any other Survival Clause, this provision shall survive any termination of this agreement for a period of five (5) years.*

Such embedded survival terms may be necessary depending on the unique details of the agreement and the provisions requiring extended enforcement.

Time Periods for Survival:

Some survival clauses establish specific time periods during which the provisions must be observed. These time periods may be fixed (e.g., five years) or may end upon the occurrence of a specific event (e.g., when the confidential information becomes publicly available).

Indefinite Survival:

In some cases, survival clauses may provide for indefinite survival, meaning that the provisions remain in effect permanently. However, the enforceability of such clauses may be limited by laws that protect individuals' rights to work and provide for themselves.

Interpretation of Survival Clauses
The interpretation of survival clauses can vary by jurisdiction. Some courts have ruled that survival clauses can act as statutes of limitations, restricting the time period during which a party can bring legal action for a breach of contract. Therefore, it is crucial to carefully word survival clauses to avoid unintended consequences.

Best Practices for Drafting Survival Clauses

- Clarity: Ensure that the wording of the survival clause is clear and unambiguous.
- Specificity: Tailor the survival clause to the specific needs and circumstances of the agreement.
- Jurisdictional Awareness: Be aware of how survival clauses are interpreted in the relevant jurisdiction.
- Legal Consultation: Consider consulting with a legal professional to ensure that the survival clause is properly drafted and enforceable.

Why Survivable Terms Matter

Government contracts can be lengthy and complex, with NDAs often having a shorter term than the underlying contract. When a NDA terminates, the parties may mistakenly believe all obligations have lapsed. Without a Survivable Terms Clause, vital provisions protecting confidential information, outlining dispute resolution procedures, or establishing indemnification responsibilities may inadvertently expire. This could leave a prime contractor exposed to significant risks, including the potential misuse of proprietary data by subcontractors.

Protecting Contractors with a Survivable Terms Clause

By explicitly stating which terms will survive termination, you are able to provide clarity and certainty. Confidentiality obligations, for instance, should always continue post-termination to ensure the ongoing protection of sensitive information. Similarly, provisions related to intellectual property rights, non-solicitation of employees, and the governing law for disputes should endure.

The clause should also address the return or destruction of confidential information upon termination. Without this, subcontractors might retain sensitive data indefinitely, posing a risk to the prime contractor.

Here is an example of an Industry Standard Survivable Terms Clause

> ***Survival of Terms***
> *Unless otherwise stated within this document, the obligations of the parties under sections [list specific sections or articles, for example., 2 (Confidential Information), 3 (Governing Law), 7 (Return of Information), 11 (Remedies), 15 (Indemnification)] will survive the termination or expiration of this Agreement. Upon termination, the receiving party will promptly return all confidential*

information of the disclosing party in its possession, custody, or control, including all copies and derivatives thereof.

Note: the above example, places the burden to "promptly return all confidential information… in its possession, custody or control, including all copies" on the Receiving Party without any written request from the Disclosing Party. In this clause, the return of information is an automatic function to be performed immediately upon termination or expiration of the agreement. As such, the Receiving Party must have robust management, tracking, and reporting systems in place to ensure smooth compliance with the requirements of this clause.

Which Clauses Should Survive?

Every company and situation is unique, and contracting professionals must carefully evaluate the specific circumstances that may influence their needs. It is essential to determine which clauses should appropriately survive beyond the termination of the NDA based on the particular requirements of the agreement and the relationship.

The specific clauses that should survive termination can, and will, vary depending on the nature of the information being protected and the specific terms of the NDA. However, as a general rule, the following is a list of clauses that are generally considered for inclusion as clauses that will survive the termination of a Non-Disclosure Agreement (NDA):

1. **Confidentiality Obligations:** The obligation to keep information confidential should continue even after the agreement has terminated. This is the main purpose of an NDA.

2. **Non-Disclosure:** Similar to confidentiality obligations, requirements to not disclose certain information typically outlive the agreement itself.

3. **Non-Use Clauses:** These clauses stipulate that confidential information can only be used for the purposes defined in the NDA. Restrictions on use often survive termination.

4. **Governing Law and Jurisdiction:** Clauses specifying which laws govern the agreement and where disputes will be resolved should be survivable.

5. **Remedies/Limitations of Liability:** The availability of equitable remedies (such as injunctions or damages) for breach of the NDA should survive termination.

6. **Return/Destruction of Confidential Information:** The requirement to return or destroy confidential information upon termination should survive.

7. **Warranties/Representations:** Any warranties, representations, or promises and statements made by parties during the term of the NDA should survive termination.

8. **Indemnification:** Any indemnification obligations to compensate another party for losses or damages should continue after termination.

9. **Dispute Resolution:** Any dispute resolution provisions (such as arbitration or mediation clauses) should continue to apply.

10. **Assignment:** Any restrictions on assignment should survive termination.

11. **Survival Clauses Themselves**: Ironically, clauses that explicitly state what other terms survive termination are themselves usually survivable!

12. **Entire Agreement:** The provision stating that the NDA constitutes the entire agreement between the parties should survive.

By carefully outlining which provisions will endure beyond the agreement's termination, contractors can ensure the ongoing protection of their sensitive information, clarity in dispute resolution, and the continuation of vital obligations.

Companion Clauses

The Survivability Clause must work in harmony with the following Companion Clauses to produce an effective NDA:

Companion Clauses	Why It's Important
Standards of Care	Sets clear obligations for the receiving party to protect the information shared.
Choice of Law	Specifies the legal framework and venue for resolving disputes.
Return of Proprietary Information	Ensures confidential information is returned or destroyed when the NDA ends.
Remedies for Breach	Provides recourse if a breach occurs during the term of the NDA.
Severability	Ensures that if one part of the NDA is found invalid or unenforceable, the remainder of the agreement remains intact.

Companion Clauses	Why It's Important
Termination	Provides an exit mechanism for ending the NDA.

ENTIRE AGREEMENT

The Entire Agreement clause provides clarity, limits disputes, and ensures that the agreement reflects the true intent of the parties. When paired with companion clauses, it becomes part of a comprehensive framework that protects both prime contractors and subcontractors.

Why the Entire Agreement Clause Is Necessary

The Entire Agreement clause establishes that the NDA is the complete and final agreement between the parties concerning the subject matter. It prevents misunderstandings by ensuring that:

1. **Only Written Terms Apply:** Oral promises, or prior agreements are excluded.

2. **Future Modifications Are Controlled:** Changes must be explicitly documented in writing.

Without this clause, either party could claim the existence of additional obligations or terms not included in the signed NDA, leading to legal disputes and uncertainty. For prime contractors and subcontractors, this is especially critical when the protection of company sensitive information is at stake.

What the Entire Agreement Clause Should Address

An effective Entire Agreement clause should include the following key elements:

1. Exclusion of Prior Understandings:
The clause should clearly state that the NDA supersedes all prior agreements, negotiations, or understandings related to the subject matter.

2. **Control Over Modifications:**
To maintain clarity, the clause should specify that any amendments or additions must be made in writing and signed by authorized representatives of both parties.

3. **Limitation to the Subject Matter:**
The clause should restrict its scope to the matters explicitly addressed in the NDA, avoiding unintended overlap with other contracts or agreements between the parties.

4. **Protection Against Implied Terms:**
By stating that no unwritten or implied terms exist, the clause ensures that the agreement's obligations and rights are limited to what is explicitly documented.

Why Contractors Should Be Concerned About the Content

Despite its simplicity, the Entire Agreement clause must be carefully drafted. Contractors should pay close attention to:

1. **Unintended Exclusions:**
If prior agreements or understandings are relevant, they must be explicitly incorporated or referenced in the NDA.

2. **Conflict with Other Agreements:**
Overlapping clauses in other contracts (e.g., teaming agreements or master service agreements) can create ambiguity. The Entire Agreement clause should state whether it complements or replaces related provisions.

3. **Vague Language:**
Ambiguous wording can lead to disputes about whether specific obligations or rights are covered. Clarity is essential to ensure enforceability.

Here is an example of an Industry-Standard clause that reflects best practices, providing clarity and protection for both parties:

Entire Agreement:
This Agreement embodies all the understandings between the Parties concerning the subject matter of this Agreement. This Agreement merges all prior discussions and writings between the parties as to confidentiality of information related to the subject. No other unwritten or implied terms exist. Neither of the parties shall be bound by any conditions, warranties, or representations with respect to confidentiality of information other than as expressly provided in this Agreement, or as set forth in a subsequent written amendment signed by the parties.

Companion Clauses to the Entire Agreement Clause

The Entire Agreement clause works in conjunction with other provisions to ensure a well-rounded and enforceable NDA:

Companion Clauses	Why It's Important
Standards of Care	Sets clear obligations for the receiving party to protect the information shared.
Choice of Law	Specifies the legal framework and venue for resolving disputes.
Return of Proprietary Information	Ensures confidential information is returned or destroyed when the NDA ends.
Remedies for Breach	Provides recourse if a breach occurs during the term of the NDA.

Part III
Negotiation and Management

Chapter 5
Negotiation Strategies

Introduction

Contracting professionals pour significant time and energy into negotiating the substantive provisions of NDAs and contracts. Yet, some terms are often overlooked or undervalued, perceived as being less important or risky. This is particularly true for boilerplate clauses - those standard provisions that appear in NDA after NDA.

Interestingly, while everyone has an opinion about what constitutes a boilerplate clause, there's little agreement on a precise definition. Many assume these clauses are carved in stone, and therefore non-negotiable.

Unfortunately, the sheer length and complexity of some boilerplate clauses can be intimidating. Clauses steeped in dense legal language or highly technical jargon are often avoided altogether because they are difficult to understand for non-legal professionals. They often use archaic terms, long-winded sentences, and convoluted phrasing, making it hard for readers to grasp the meaning or implications without significant effort. This lack of clarity creates uncertainty, leaving parties unsure of what they're agreeing to.

To effectively negotiate the terms and clauses of an NDA, you must first develop a clear understanding of their intent, the benefits, and potential pitfalls. Without this foundational knowledge, it's impossible to confidently advocate for your organization's interests or mitigate the potential risks.

At the most basic level, the clauses within a NDA form the structural foundation of these agreements, clearly outlining the rights, obligations, and expectations of all parties involved. As a government contracting professional, you play a vital role in safeguarding proprietary data while laying the groundwork for effective collaborations that adhere to strict federal regulations.

Whether you are a prime contractor, subcontractor, information recipient, or discloser, fully understanding the clauses contained within a NDA is key to tailoring the agreement to your unique circumstances and leverage points.

Why Clauses Matter

Each clause in a NDA carries weight—these are not "check-the-box" provisions. The specific language of these terms determines the strength and enforceability of your agreement. For example:

- Are you prepared to maintain and track the confidentiality of information you receive in compliance with the NDA's terms?

- Have you considered whether you are the sole party receiving sensitive data or if the disclosing party is sharing it with competitors?

- Do the clauses adequately address remedies for breaches or provide the necessary flexibility for mutual disclosures?

These questions underline the importance of drafting clauses that not only align with legal standards but also reflect the realities of your operational environment.

Key Themes in Negotiation

When negotiating NDA terms, the balance of power and the nature of the relationship between the parties play critical roles. Ask yourself:

- Are you disclosing information or primarily receiving it?
- Is the disclosure mutual, or is one party the primary custodian of sensitive data?
- What is the purpose of the NDA?
- What type of information is being shared, and why?
- Who are the parties involved, and what are their priorities?

These factors influence the strength and flexibility of the clauses you need and by aligning the NDA's clauses with the specific goals of the relationship, you can focus on negotiating terms that matter most to both parties. For example, disclosing parties often require stringent protection standards and detailed tracking, while recipients may push for reasonable limits on liability and duration.

Prioritize Key Clauses

Not all clauses carry the same weight in every negotiation. Identify the clauses that are most critical to your organization's interests. Typically, these include:

- **Definition of Confidential Information:** Ensure it accurately covers the information you need to protect without being overly broad or ambiguous.

- **Term and Duration:** Negotiate a timeframe that aligns with the nature of the information and its relevance over time.

- **Return or Destruction of Information:** Establish clear obligations for handling confidential information after the NDA ends.

- **Affiliates and Third Parties:** Depending on the corporate organizational structure of your firm, the disclosing party's sensitive information may be stored in a way that allows access by your parent organization or other affiliated legal entities.

By focusing on the most impactful clauses, you can direct your efforts where they matter most and avoid unnecessary delays over less significant terms.

Acknowledge Red Flags

Red flags are the clauses, terms, or anticipated outcomes that serve as crucial early warning indicators, signaling potential risks, misalignments, or hidden complexities. Rather than viewing these signals as mere obstacles, skilled negotiators recognize them as valuable sources of strategic insight. By addressing red flags proactively, they can prevent costly misunderstandings, safeguard organizational interests, and reduce legal and financial vulnerabilities.

Whether you are a prime contractor or a subcontractor, staying vigilant for red flags is essential to identifying opportunities for strategic negotiation. These moments can help you mitigate significant risks while advancing your objectives.

A Strategic Approach to Negotiation

Addressing the content of specific clauses during negotiation is not about fostering adversarial interactions but about cultivating transparent, mutually advantageous agreements. Savvy negotiators view these discussions as opportunities for collaborative problem-solving, leveraging them to promote deeper understanding, clearer communication, and more resilient contractual terms. The aim isn't to eliminate all risks (an unrealistic goal) but to design adaptable, well-defined agreements that protect key interests while building trust and mutual respect. This approach lays the groundwork for strong, enduring relationships and a potential fruitful contracting environment..

Use a Collaborative Approach

Effective NDA negotiations require a collaborative mindset. While protecting your interests is essential, acknowledging the other party's concerns fosters goodwill and leads to quicker resolutions.

For example, if the other party objects to the length of confidentiality obligations, consider offering a compromise by tying the duration to specific events, such as the conclusion of a government procurement cycle. Collaborative negotiation builds trust and sets the tone for the broader business relationship.

Be Prepared to Justify Your Position

Negotiations often stall when one party doesn't understand the rationale behind a particular clause. Be ready to explain the purpose of each term and how it aligns with your organization's needs.

For instance, if you require a clause that limits the use of confidential information to a specific project, explain how this protects proprietary data while still allowing the other party to fulfill their obligations. By framing your requests as reasonable and necessary, you can reduce resistance and find common ground.

Leverage Companion Clauses

Companion clauses are interconnected provisions that rely on each other for effectiveness. During negotiations, use these relationships to strengthen your position. For example:

- If the other party seeks to expand the scope of Exceptions to Confidentiality, insist on a robust Notice of Disclosure clause to ensure you're informed of any exceptions they invoke.

- If they request a shorter confidentiality term, negotiate stricter Return or Destruction of Information obligations to mitigate potential risks.

By showing how changes to one clause impact its companions, you demonstrate your expertise and reinforce the importance of maintaining balance across the agreement.

Avoid Boilerplate Overuse

While pre-approved templates can expedite negotiations, relying too heavily on boilerplate language can lead to clauses that don't align with the specific context of your NDA. Review standard terms critically and adjust them to reflect the unique needs of the situation.

For example, if your template includes a one-size-fits-all Indemnification clause, tailor it to address the specific risks associated with the relationship, such as data breaches or unauthorized disclosures. Customizing these terms shows attention to detail and reduces the likelihood of disputes later.

Know When to Escalate

Some negotiations involve complex or non-standard terms that require additional input. Recognize when to escalate discussions to your legal team or other stakeholders.

For instance:

- Clauses involving intellectual property rights often intersect with broader contractual obligations. Consult experts to ensure your NDA doesn't inadvertently compromise those rights.
- If the other party proposes a governing law clause that introduces unfamiliar legal risks, involve your legal team to assess the implications.

Knowing when to escalate ensures that you address nuanced issues without derailing the negotiation process.

Use Real-World Examples to Build Consensus

When negotiating contentious clauses, examples can be powerful tools for building understanding and agreement. Reference industry practices, case studies, or prior agreements to illustrate why a particular term is reasonable. For instance: If the other party questions the necessity of a Remedies for Breach clause, cite examples of disputes where the absence of such remedies led to significant financial losses.

Grounding your position in real-world scenarios can help bridge gaps in understanding and encourage resolution.

Document and Track Negotiation Changes

Throughout the negotiation process, keep detailed records of proposed changes, counteroffers, and agreed terms. This documentation not only ensures transparency but also provides a reference point for future agreements.

Using a commercially available contract management tool or system can streamline this process, allowing you to track revisions, maintain version control, and generate a final document efficiently.

Plan for Long-Term Success

NDAs are often the starting point for broader business relationships. Negotiating in good faith and ensuring the agreement is fair and enforceable lays a strong foundation for future collaboration.

To that end, ensure the final NDA is practical and realistic for both parties to uphold. Overly aggressive terms may secure short-term gains but risk souring the relationship or leading to non-compliance down the line.

Putting Knowledge Into Action

It's essential to analyze your specific situation — whether as a prime contractor or subcontractor — and identify the distinctive potential issues that may arise. By being mindful of these risks and opportunities, you can tailor your approach to uncover and address the factors most critical to your organization's success.

The key to effective negotiation is taking action. If you don't ask for better terms, you're unlikely not going to receive them. Skilled negotiators understand that asking for improvements — whether it's clearer definitions, stronger protections, or more favorable terms — is not only a right but a responsibility. Even small adjustments can make a significant difference in mitigating risks and aligning the agreement with your strategic goals.

Conclusion

Negotiation is not about accepting what's offered at face value but about collaboratively working together to shape an agreement that reflects a balance of risks and rewards that works for both parties.

Mastering the art of NDA negotiation requires preparation, clarity, and a strategic mindset. By understanding the purpose of each clause, prioritizing key terms, and approaching discussions collaboratively, you can craft agreements that protect your organization's interests while fostering positive relationships.

Remember, every negotiation is an opportunity to demonstrate your expertise, build trust, and set the stage for success. With the strategies outlined in this chapter, you're well on your way to becoming a true NDA Wizard.

Chapter 6
Avoiding Overreach

Introduction

All NDAs are not created equal. Overly broad, unrealistic, or one-sided agreements, commonly referred to as "overreaching" NDAs, can create unnecessary legal risks, operational inefficiencies, and strained partnerships.

While the intent of a NDA is to protect information, pushing for overly restrictive or impractical terms can backfire. Clauses that impose unreasonable obligations, ambiguous requirements, or disproportionate burdens on one party often lead to delays, resistance, and unenforceable agreements. In government contracting, your compliance with regulations like FAR, DFARS, and export control laws are non-negotiable, and the consequences of overreach are even more significant.

Avoiding overreach requires a careful balance. NDAs must provide meaningful protections while remaining practical to implement and fair to all parties involved. In this chapter, we will explore what constitutes overreach, why it is problematic, and how contracting professionals can develop agreements that are strong, enforceable, and operationally sound.

What is Overreach in NDAs?

Overreach occurs when a NDA includes terms that are unnecessarily broad, overly restrictive, or impractical to enforce. These terms often go beyond what is needed to protect confidential information and instead create unintended burdens or risks for the parties involved.

The most common examples of overreach include vague definitions of confidential information, indefinite confidentiality obligations, and impractical compliance requirements. For instance, some NDAs attempt to classify all information exchanged between parties as confidential, regardless of whether it is sensitive, proprietary, or already publicly available. Others impose perpetual obligations for non-trade secret data or restrict the use of information so severely that it interferes with contract performance or proposal development.

Overreach can also manifest itself in one-sided terms that disproportionately favor the disclosing party. Clauses that impose excessive penalties, unrealistic monitoring obligations, or rigid disclosure restrictions can discourage collaboration, delay negotiations, and ultimately erode trust between the parties.

Why Overreach is Problematic

Overreaching NDAs often create more problems than they solve. One of the primary issues with overreach is unenforceability. Courts are unlikely to enforce NDAs that contain unreasonable or overly broad clauses. For example, an indefinite confidentiality period for general business information may be viewed as excessive, particularly when the value of that data diminishes over time. When courts strike down these clauses, the NDA may lose its protective power entirely, leaving sensitive information exposed.

Operational inefficiencies are another significant consequence. NDAs with impractical terms can create compliance challenges and unnecessary administrative burdens. For instance, requiring information to be disclosed only in hard-copy format or limiting access to an unreasonably small group can disrupt workflows and slow progress. In government contracting, where time-sensitive proposals and complex subcontractor relationships are the norm, these restrictions can significantly impact performance.

Overreach can also stifle collaboration. Subcontractors, teaming partners, and vendors may be reluctant to engage in a project if they feel the NDA places an unfair burden on them. Excessive restrictions or penalties can create a perception of distrust, making it harder to foster open, cooperative relationships.

Finally, overreach damages relationships by creating tension between parties. Instead of serving as a foundation for trust, an overly aggressive NDA sends a message of distrust and suspicion. This harms long-term partnerships, which are critical for success in government contracting.

Recognizing Signs of Overreach

Overreach often stems from an overzealous attempt to protect information but can be identified by reviewing the NDA for key warning signs. Clauses that classify all information as confidential, regardless of its relevance or sensitivity, are a red flag. Similarly, terms that impose indefinite confidentiality obligations for non-trade secret data should be examined closely.

Another common indicator is a lack of balance in obligations. If the receiving party is expected to carry all the compliance burdens, such as ensuring that third-party subcontractors adhere to confidentiality terms without reasonable oversight mechanisms, the NDA is likely one-sided. Similarly, overly restrictive Permitted Use clauses that limit how information can be shared—even when necessary for contract performance—can create operational challenges.

Language that lacks specificity is also problematic. Vague definitions, ambiguous standards (e.g., requiring "absolute protection" instead of "reasonable efforts"), and unclear remedies for breach introduce uncertainty and increase the risk of disputes.

Professionals should approach NDAs with an eye toward identifying these signs early. By addressing potential overreach before the agreement is finalized, parties can avoid unnecessary conflicts and delays.

Balancing Protection and Practicality

The key to avoiding overreach in NDAs is to strike a balance between protecting confidential information and ensuring that the terms are fair, practical, and enforceable. Government contracting professionals must evaluate each NDA in the context of the relationship, the nature of the information being shared, and the regulatory environment.

First, NDAs should clearly and narrowly define what constitutes confidential information. Instead of including broad, all-encompassing definitions, focus on specific categories such as technical data, bid and proposal pricing, financial reports, and CUI. Exclude publicly available information, independently developed data, and information obtained through lawful means.

Second, the duration of confidentiality obligations should be reasonable and aligned with the value of the protected information. While trade secrets may warrant indefinite protection, most general business information does not. Three to five years is a common and practical standard for most non-trade secret data.

Permitted Use clauses should support, rather than hinder, business operations. The receiving party should be allowed to use the information exchanged for the clearly defined purposes, such as proposal development, subcontractor performance, or compliance with federal requirements. Include provisions that allow disclosures to employees, subcontractors, or consultants who need access to fulfill these obligations, provided they are bound by similar confidentiality terms.

Finally, ensure that remedies for breach are fair and proportionate. Excessive penalties or one-sided indemnification clauses can create resistance and prolong negotiations. Instead, include reasonable remedies such as injunctive relief to prevent further unauthorized disclosures and monetary damages tied to actual harm.

Conclusion

Overreach in NDAs often results from an excessive focus on protection without regard for practicality, balance, or enforceability. While the intent may be to safeguard sensitive information, overly broad, ambiguous, or unreasonable terms can create unintended risks, strain partnerships, and disrupt operations.

By recognizing the signs of overreach and focusing on clear, fair, and practical terms, government contracting professionals can draft NDAs that achieve their intended purpose without creating unnecessary burdens. A well-crafted NDA protects confidential information, supports regulatory compliance, and fosters trust—ultimately serving as a tool for collaboration and success in government contracting.

Chapter 7
Common Pitfalls

Introduction

When executed properly, NDAs provide a clear framework for confidentiality, ensuring compliance with federal requirements. However, even seasoned professionals can stumble during the drafting, review, or negotiation phases. These missteps often result in unenforceable agreements, unintended risks, or disputes that compromise the very information the NDA was designed to protect.

This chapter explores the most common pitfalls in NDAs, explains why they occur, and offers practical strategies to avoid them. By addressing these areas, government contracting professionals can mitigate risk, ensure enforceability, and maintain NDAs as reliable mechanisms for protecting confidential information.

Vague or Overbroad Definitions of Confidential Information

One of the most frequent pitfalls in NDAs is failing to define "Confidential Information" or "Proprietary Information" with sufficient clarity and precision. NDAs often include overly broad definitions, attempting to cover all information related to a project, or provide vague terms that leave parties uncertain about what information is protected.

This lack of precision creates ambiguity that courts may find unenforceable, while overly broad definitions place an unreasonable burden on the receiving party. Moreover, operational confusion may arise when neither party can clearly identify what requires protection.

To avoid this, NDAs should provide a clear, specific definition of confidential information, often by identifying distinct categories such as "technical data," "financial information," or "proprietary software." When appropriate, require confidential materials to be clearly marked or designated in writing to ensure there is no ambiguity.

Example:
"Confidential Information includes any technical, financial, business, or other proprietary information disclosed in written, or electronic, form and clearly marked as confidential."

Missing or Unrealistic Term or Duration

Another common pitfall is failing to specify the duration of confidentiality obligations or imposing indefinite terms for all types of information. While trade secrets warrant indefinite protection, general proprietary information does not.

Without clear terms, courts may deem indefinite durations unreasonable, rendering the NDA unenforceable. Excessively long terms also create operational challenges, particularly for non-critical information.

NDAs should include reasonable timeframes (typically three to five years) for general confidential information, while specifying that trade secrets remain protected indefinitely. In such situations, it is important that the negotiator understands the slight, but clearly distinguishable differences between proprietary information and information that qualifies as Trade Secrets.

Trade Secrets are a subset of proprietary information that qualifies for legal protects under trade secret laws such as the Uniform Trade Secrets Act (UTSA) in the U.S. or the Defend Trade Secrets Act (DTSA) at the federal level. The key distinction lies in the economic value derived from secrecy and the reasonable efforts to maintain secrecy. If information meets these two criteria, it may be classified as a trade secret under statutes like the UTSA or DTSA. If it does not meet these criteria but is still considered private or confidential, it remains proprietary or confidential information.

> *Example:*
> *"The confidentiality obligations under this Agreement shall remain in effect for five (5) years following disclosure, except for trade secrets, which shall remain confidential indefinitely."*

Failure to Address Permitted Disclosures

NDAs that lack provisions for permitted disclosures can create significant problems when legal obligations, such as court orders, audits, or regulatory requirements, mandate disclosure of confidential information.

Without a clear clause, the receiving party may inadvertently breach the agreement or face uncertainty about how to comply with both the NDA and legal demands.

To address this, NDAs should explicitly allow disclosures required by law, court order, or government regulations, while requiring the receiving party to provide prompt written notice to the disclosing party, when legally permissible.

> *Example:*
> *"The Receiving Party may disclose Confidential Information as required by law, court order, or regulatory obligations, provided it gives the Disclosing Party prompt written notice to allow for protective action."*

Overly Restrictive Permitted Use

Some NDAs restrict the receiving party's use of proprietary information so severely that it interferes with legitimate operations, such as performing contract obligations or preparing proposals. Overly strict language can cause inefficiencies or ambiguity, leaving parties unsure of what is allowed.

To avoid this, NDAs should clearly define the specific purpose for which confidential information may be used, such as "contract performance" or "proposal development." Additionally, the agreement should permit disclosure to employees, subcontractors, or agents who have a legitimate need to know.

> *Example:*
> *"The Receiving Party shall use the Confidential Information solely for the purpose of [specific purpose] and shall disclose it only to those employees or agents who have a need to know."*

Neglecting Remedies for Breach

NDAs often omit essential details about remedies for breach, leaving the disclosing party with limited recourse in the event of unauthorized disclosure. Without clear enforcement provisions, disputes may become prolonged, costly, and difficult to resolve.

To ensure enforceability, NDAs should explicitly include provisions for injunctive relief, monetary damages, and recovery of reasonable legal fees. This provides the disclosing party with the tools to stop breaches quickly and recover losses.

> *Example:*
> *"The Disclosing Party shall be entitled to injunctive relief, monetary damages, and reasonable attorney's fees in the event of a breach of this Agreement."*

Ignoring Choice of Law and Jurisdiction

NDAs that omit a governing law or jurisdiction clause can create uncertainty about which state or federal laws apply, resulting in costly jurisdictional disputes. Without an agreed-upon venue, courts may apply laws that are unfavorable to one party, delaying enforcement and increasing legal expenses.

To avoid this, NDAs should specify the governing law and jurisdiction where disputes will be resolved. For efficiency, parties may also consider alternative dispute resolution (ADR) options, such as arbitration or mediation.

> *Example:*
> *"This Agreement shall be governed by the laws of the State of [State], and any disputes arising hereunder shall be resolved in the courts of [State or specified venue]."*

Overreaching Obligations to Affiliates and Subcontractors

Some NDAs impose unreasonable obligations on the receiving party to ensure compliance by affiliates, subcontractors, or third parties. Such overreach places an undue operational burden, as the receiving party may lack control over all third-party actions.

To address this, NDAs should require the receiving party to make reasonable efforts to bind affiliates and subcontractors to confidentiality obligations. Disclosures should be limited to parties with a legitimate need to know.

> *Example:*
> *"The Receiving Party shall ensure that any third-party recipients of Confidential Information are*

bound by confidentiality obligations no less stringent than those set forth herein."

Conclusion

Avoiding common pitfalls in NDAs requires careful attention to both legal and practical considerations. By ensuring clear definitions, reasonable durations, and enforceable remedies, professionals can create NDAs that are fair, effective, and aligned with the realities of government contracting.

A well-drafted NDA not only fosters trust but also protects critical information, facilitating smoother collaborations and minimizing risk. Proactively addressing these potential challenges will position government contracting professionals to secure their confidential information while maintaining operational efficiency.

Chapter 8
Compliance and Enforcement

Introduction

The effectiveness of any NDA depends not only on the strength of the negotiated clauses but also on the parties' ability to ensure compliance and take enforcement actions when breaches occur. Both the disclosing and receiving parties must establish robust systems to ensure NDAs are honored. Additionally, enforcement mechanisms must be clearly understood and consistently applied.

This chapter examines the dual responsibilities of compliance and enforcement from the perspectives of both the **disclosing parties** (who share the information) and the **receiving parties** (who must protect the information). It also highlights the vital role of record-keeping, explores options for enforcement, and discusses the consequences of breaching an NDA.

Compliance: The Responsibility of the Receiving Party

The receiving party, whether a prime contractor, subcontractor, or consultant, bears the primary responsibility for protecting confidential information. Compliance begins the moment a NDA is signed and requires ongoing diligence. Failure to fully comply with the negotiated terms of an NDA, even unintentionally, can result in severe legal and reputational consequences.

Establishing Clear Procedures:

Receiving parties must implement clear, written procedures for handling confidential information. These include:

- Identifying authorized personnel who may access the information.
- Limiting access to information on a **need-to-know basis**.
- Securing physical and electronic records through encryption, firewalls, or restricted file-sharing systems.

For subcontractors, compliance is particularly critical since they are often entrusted with sensitive technical and financial data necessary for government proposals. Prime contractors, as stewards of the government's interest, are responsible for ensuring their subcontractors comply with NDAs.

Monitoring and Training:

Compliance is not static. The receiving party must continuously train employees on the importance of NDAs and the consequences of breaches. For example:

- Regular **compliance training** ensures employees recognize what constitutes confidential information.

- **Internal audits** can verify that data security protocols are being followed.

Example Scenario:

A prime contractor shares proprietary pricing information with a subcontractor under an NDA. To ensure compliance, the subcontractor limits access to the information to a single secure server and logs all access attempts. Internal audits confirm that no unauthorized personnel accessed the data.

The Importance of Record-Keeping for Enforcement

NDAs are only as strong as your ability to enforce them. For disclosing parties (whether prime contractors or subcontractors)

record-keeping is critical to proving a breach occurred and determining liability.

Meticulous records must document:

1. **What confidential information was disclosed:** Describe the nature, scope, and form (e.g., documents, verbal exchanges) of the information.

2. **How it was disclosed:** Specify the method—meetings, secure emails, or physical handovers.

3. **Who received it:** Identify the individuals or entities with authorized access to the information.

4. **When it was returned or destroyed:** Maintain logs confirming the recipient complied with return/destruction requirements.

Enforcing an NDA: Steps and Options for the Disclosing Party

Even with strong clauses and diligent compliance, breaches can still occur. When they do, the disclosing party has several enforcement options:

1. **Investigation and Evidence Collection:** The first step in enforcement is confirming that a breach occurred and gathering evidence. Key considerations include:
   - Was the confidential information accidentally or intentionally shared?
   - Is the leaked information easily available through other public sources?
   - Can you prove the recipient caused the breach?

2. **Informal Resolution:** Before pursuing legal action, many disclosing parties opt for informal resolution. This may involve:
   - Sending a **cease-and-desist letter** demanding that the recipient stop further use or disclosure.
   - Requesting the recipient return or destroy the information immediately.

3. **Legal Enforcement:** If informal resolution fails, the disclosing party may pursue legal remedies. An NDA, when executed properly, is legally binding and enforceable. Legal options include:
   - **Injunctive Relief:** A court order to stop the recipient from further using or sharing the confidential information.
   - **Monetary Damages:** Compensation for financial losses caused by the breach. This may include actual damages, lost profits, or punitive damages in egregious cases.
   - **Specific Performance:** Court enforcement requiring the recipient to comply with the NDA's terms, such as returning or destroying the confidential information.

Enforcement Pathways

Enforcement Option	Description	When Used
Informal Resolution	Cease-and-desist letter or mutual resolution.	Minor breaches or accidental leaks.
Injunctive Relief	Court-ordered prevention of further use/disclosure.	Ongoing or imminent misuse.

Enforcement Option	Description	When Used
Monetary Damages	Compensation for financial harm caused by the breach.	Demonstrable financial losses.
Specific Performance	Enforces actions such as data return/destruction.	Noncompliance with NDA terms.

Consequences of Violating an NDA

Violating a NDA carries serious consequences that vary depending on the severity of the breach, the harm caused, and the parties' contractual language. Consequences include:

1. **Financial Penalties:** The breaching party may be liable for damages, including:
   - **Actual damages** (e.g., loss of business, financial harm).
   - **Punitive damages** in cases involving willful misconduct.

2. **Reputational Damage:** For subcontractors and prime contractors alike, breaching a NDA can tarnish professional reputations, making it difficult to win future contracts or team with other firms.

3. **Termination of Contracts:** A breach may give the disclosing party grounds to terminate existing contracts or agreements with the violating party.

Example Scenario:

A subcontractor inadvertently leaks technical designs shared under an NDA. The breach causes financial harm to the prime contractor, who files a lawsuit seeking injunctive relief and damages. The subcontractor is ordered to pay $100,000 in damages and is disqualified from future teaming opportunities.

Compliance and Enforcement: Prime Contractors vs. Subcontractors

From both perspectives, compliance and enforcement efforts must align to ensure sensitive government and business information is protected.

- **Prime Contractor Perspective:**
  Prime contractors must ensure their subcontractors comply with NDAs to avoid liability under federal requirements. They may:
    o Mandate subcontractors conduct compliance audits.
    o Enforce strict reporting and record-keeping requirements.

- **Subcontractor Perspective:**
  Subcontractors, while often in the receiving party role, must prove their ability to protect confidential information. Compliance failures can jeopardize their credibility and future contracts.

Conclusion

Compliance and enforcement are two sides of the same coin. While the receiving party must establish robust systems to safeguard confidential information, the disclosing party must remain vigilant in monitoring, record-keeping, and enforcing NDAs when breaches occur. NDAs are only as strong as the processes in place to uphold them. For both prime contractors and subcontractors in the government contracting space, prioritizing compliance and understanding enforcement mechanisms ensures that NDAs fulfill their intended purpose: protecting sensitive and valuable information.

Chapter 9
System Management

Introduction

Signing a NDA is more than acknowledging an agreement—it is a commitment to implementing robust systems for safeguarding, tracking, reporting, returning, and potentially destroying proprietary information. This commitment often exceeds the expectations of many who see NDAs as mere paperwork. Success requires:

- Establishing clear internal systems to track confidential information.
- Identifying who within your organization has access to sensitive data.
- Ensuring your team enforces the same protections on the protected information you receive as you enact for protecting your own sensitive information.

Successfully managing the operational demands that are required for compliance is a vital yet often underestimated aspect of the contract lifecycle. Though NDAs may appear straightforward, inefficiencies, poor organization, and a lack of standardization can lead to delays, compliance risks, and missed obligations.

To ensure robust protection, contractors must adopt a comprehensive NDA management approach that includes:

- **Implementing technological safeguards (e.g., encryption, access controls)**
  This means using advanced technologies to protect sensitive information from unauthorized access. Examples include encrypting data so it's unreadable without a key, setting up

access controls to restrict information only to authorized individuals, and employing secure file-sharing platforms. These safeguards act as a first line of defense against data breaches or leaks.

- **Conducting regular employee training on confidentiality obligations**
This involves educating employees about their responsibilities regarding confidential information. Training should cover the terms of NDAs, the importance of maintaining confidentiality, and the potential consequences of breaches. Regular training ensures that employees are aware of current best practices and reinforces a culture of accountability.

- **Establishing clear internal policies and processes for handling sensitive information**
This refers to creating structured guidelines for how sensitive information should be managed within the organization. Policies might include designating specific personnel to handle confidential documents, defining procedures for document sharing or destruction, and implementing checks for compliance. Clear policies help ensure consistency and reduce the likelihood of errors.

- **Monitoring regulatory changes and ensuring compliance**
This involves staying up-to-date with changes in laws or regulations that affect how sensitive information must be handled. For instance, government contracting may involve specific confidentiality requirements under federal acquisition regulations (FAR). Contractors need to adapt their NDA management and overall practices to comply with these evolving standards, thereby avoiding legal risks.

An effective NDA management strategy provides the necessary framework to protect sensitive information and yet encourage productive partnerships, by streamlining processes, reducing risk, and ensuring that confidential information remains secure across all business operations.

By implementing standardized workflows, leveraging technology, training teams, and ensuring compliance, contracting professionals can efficiently manage NDAs while focusing on delivering value.

Develop a Standardized NDA Process

A standardized NDA process provides consistency, reduces errors, and accelerates the review and execution of agreements. Without clear procedures, NDAs can become bottlenecks that delay partnerships, subcontractor engagements, or teaming agreements.

To improve consistency, organizations should develop pre-approved NDA templates for common scenarios, such as prime-subcontractor NDAs, vendor engagements, or proposal collaborations. A defined workflow for review and approval should outline the necessary steps, key stakeholders—including legal, compliance, and program management—and timelines for each stage of the process. For instance, setting a 48-hour window for legal reviews can help eliminate unnecessary delays.

Additionally, escalation procedures should be established for handling non-standard terms or complex negotiations. A clear escalation protocol ensures efficient resolution while maintaining appropriate risk oversight.

A comprehensive NDA management system should track critical details for each transaction such as what information was received, when it was received, who provided it, who has access to it, protection period requirements, what program does the NDA support, and what the return or destruction requirements are. For example, immediately upon receiving another party's protected information, organizations should "firewall" it, restricting access to only authorized personnel as dictated by the applicable agreement.

Leverage Technology for NDA Management

Relying on manual processes for NDA management often results in version control issues, missed deadlines, and disorganized records. Many of the commercially available contract management software products offer a powerful solution by automating key aspects of the NDA lifecycle, improving efficiency, accuracy, and compliance. Regardless of what route you pursue, using a management system that is based on advanced technologies to protect sensitive information from unauthorized access should be the foundation of your NDA management system. Examples include encrypting data so it's unreadable without a key, setting up access controls to restrict information only to authorized individuals, and employing secure file-sharing platforms. These safeguards act as a first line of defense against data breaches or leaks.

Tools such as DocuSign CLM, Agiloft, or Icertis streamline NDA drafting, approval workflows, and electronic signatures while maintaining centralized, searchable storage. These platforms also automate reminders for key milestones, such as NDA expirations or deliverables, and maintain audit trails that ensure transparency and accountability—critical elements in government contracting.

Centralizing all NDAs in a single repository further simplifies recordkeeping and ensures easy access for compliance tracking and audits.

Train Teams on NDA Policies and Responsibilities

The success of any NDA depends on the people responsible for upholding it. Misunderstanding or neglecting obligations can result in breaches that lead to financial losses, regulatory penalties, or reputational damage.

Training programs should educate teams on the fundamentals of NDAs, such as key terms (e.g., confidentiality obligations, permitted disclosures, and return of information), the consequences of breaches, and specific compliance requirements under FAR and DFARS.

Employees must understand the terms of NDAs, the proper handling of sensitive information, and the steps to take in the event of an accidental disclosure. This includes immediate documentation, internal notification, and implementing corrective actions to prevent future issues.

Role-based training can improve understanding by tailoring content to specific responsibilities ensuring that every team member understands their responsibilities, from contract negotiators to program managers.

For example, contract professionals should focus on negotiation tactics and risk identification, while program teams need to recognize and appropriately handle confidential information. Providing quick-reference guides, checklists, and templates supports day-to-day compliance and minimizes errors.

Monitor and Enforce NDA Obligations

Signing a NDA is not the end of the process; ongoing monitoring and enforcement are critical to ensuring compliance. Government contracting professionals must actively track obligations and take prompt action to address breaches or potential issues.

Using contract management tools or simple tracking systems, teams can monitor key NDA commitments, such as confidentiality periods, reporting obligations, or requirements to return or destroy proprietary information. Organizations should regularly audit compliance, particularly when dealing with subcontractors, consultants, or vendors, to ensure sensitive data is adequately protected.

In addition, organizations should establish clear breach protocols to respond quickly and effectively when issues arise. These protocols should include notification requirements, steps for investigating and containing breaches, and legal remedies such as injunctive relief or damages. Partnering with internal compliance teams can further strengthen oversight and enforcement.

Avoid Overuse of NDAs

While NDAs are valuable tools, they can be overused, creating unnecessary administrative burdens and friction in partnerships. Not every engagement or interaction warrants an NDA.

Organizations should evaluate whether a NDA is necessary based on the nature of the information being shared. For instance, NDAs are typically appropriate when disclosing proprietary technical data, engaging in teaming agreements, or sharing sensitive financial information. For low-risk situations, alternatives such as verbal agreements or protective disclaimers may suffice.

To further reduce administrative overhead, short-form NDA templates can streamline negotiations in low-risk scenarios without compromising key protections.

Maintain NDA Visibility Across the Contract Lifecycle

NDAs do not exist in isolation; they often intersect with other agreements such as teaming agreements, subcontracts, or licensing agreements. Poor visibility can lead to conflicting terms or overlooked obligations, increasing compliance risks.

To avoid this, professionals should ensure NDA terms align with related contracts (such as teaming agreements or subcontracts) particularly regarding data rights, term duration, and confidentiality obligations. Integrating NDA management into broader contract lifecycle systems helps track renewal or expiration dates, ensuring obligations are met on time. Assigning clear accountability for monitoring NDA compliance further strengthens oversight across the lifecycle.

Lessons Learned and Continuous Improvement

Improving NDA management is an ongoing effort. By analyzing past experiences and identifying areas for enhancement, organizations can make NDA processes more efficient and effective.

Conducting post-execution reviews of high-stakes NDAs can reveal challenges or inefficiencies in the workflow. These insights can then inform updates to standard templates or processes, ensuring they remain relevant to evolving business needs and regulatory requirements. Establishing feedback loops with internal teams fosters continuous improvement and helps mitigate recurring issues.

Conclusion

Effective NDA management is critical for government contracting professionals, ensuring sensitive information is protected while minimizing administrative burdens. By standardizing workflows, leveraging technology, training teams, and proactively monitoring obligations, organizations can transform NDAs into essential tools that protect information and enable smooth collaboration.

The key to success lies in balancing efficiency with compliance. With these best practices, NDAs become more than a formality—

they serve as a foundation for trust, operational clarity, and risk reduction in federal contracting.

Appendix 1
NDA Review Checklist

Non-Disclosure Agreement Checklist

		YES	NO	Notes
1	Are legal names and address of parties identified?	☐	☐	
2	Is an effective date stated?	☐	☐	
3	Is a specific purpose identified?	☐	☐	
4	Are Points of Contract identified – including phone and E-mail?	☐	☐	
5	Is Confidential Information defined?	☐	☐	
6	Are Procedures for Visual or Verbal disclosures adequately addressed?	☐	☐	
7	Are Standards for Protection stated – are they acceptable?	☐	☐	
8	Is use of Disclosed Information restricted in any manner?	☐	☐	
9	Is Assignment permitted? Notice? Consent?	☐	☐	
10	Is a duration period defined? Is it acceptable?	☐	☐	
11	Is a separate protection period appliable?	☐	☐	

	Is it acceptable?			
12	Are Warranties and licensed addressed? Are the terms acceptable?	☐	☐	
13	Are the terms for return of protected information adequately addressed?	☐	☐	
14	Is there a requirement for certificate of return or destruction of protected information?	☐	☐	
15	Is the Governing Law provision acceptable?	☐	☐	
16	Is Arbitration applicable to this agreement?	☐	☐	
17	Are remedies for breach clear and acceptable?	☐	☐	
18	Are Termination clauses included? Are they acceptable?	☐	☐	
19	Are Import/Export Requirements applicable?	☐	☐	
20	Are terms of Liability Clause Acceptable?			
21	Are the individual terms severable?	☐	☐	

#				
22	Are your rights of technical data preserved?	☐	☐	
23	Will the terms of this agreement roll into a Teaming Agreement?	☐	☐	
24	Are exclusions to protected information defined? Are they acceptable?	☐	☐	
25	Is sharing with Affiliates, Subcontractors, or Consultants permitted? Are you agreeable?	☐	☐	
26	Does the agreement provide for mutual indemnification?	☐	☐	

Notes / Items for Negotiation:

Appendix 2
Due Diligence Checklist

 Contracts Classroom

Due Diligence Checklist

Name of Effort:

Name of Firm being evaluated:

What is reason for selection of this potential Teammate?

Assessment of Competition / teams for this program?

Whose teaming agreement will be used and are there issues with

	GENERAL	YES	NO	Notes
1	Can this work contemplated to be subcontracted be performed in house?	☐	☐	
2	Have we considered developing the capability to perform the work to be	☐	☐	
3	Can we just award a purchase order after award without a Teaming	☐	☐	
4	Are there any ongoing audits, or investigations could have an impact on	☐	☐	
5	Is the company registered in SAM?	☐	☐	
6	Have the SAM records been reviewed and found acceptable?	☐	☐	

		YES	NO	Notes
7	Has the company completed any reps and certs for us in the past?	☐	☐	
8	In the past 5 years, have we teamed with this company on a procurement either as	☐	☐	
9	With reference to the NAICs code identified for this effort, is this firm a	☐	☐	
10	Does the firm meet any special SB classification? (SDVO, VO, WO, HBCU, HUBZone, SDB)	☐	☐	
11	Have we verified the Prime qualifies for any special set-aside requirements?	☐	☐	
12	Do we have any history teaming with this company on any other effort? Was the experience acceptable?	☐	☐	
13	Does the firm maintain a stable and capable workforce? Do they have a high turnover rate?	☐	☐	
14	Does the firm maintain an approved accounting system?	☐	☐	
15	Does the firm maintain an approved CPSR?	☐	☐	
16	Does the firm possess a FCL at the appropriate level?	☐	☐	
17	Is our expected "Lift" for the proposal phase acceptable? Do we have available resources and time?	☐	☐	

		YES	NO	Notes
18	Does this firm employ any individuals that may have a Personal Conflict of Interest?	☐	☐	
19	Any potential OCI with work currently being performed by this firm? Any with expected future work?	☐	☐	
20	Can any potential OCI issues be properly mitigated?	☒	☐	
CURRENT RELATIONSHIP				
21	Do we have any active contracts or purchase orders with this firm?	☐	☐	
22	What is this firm's current Vendor Rating?	☐	☐	
23	Do we have any in-active contracts or purchase orders with this firm?	☐	☐	
FINANCIAL CAPABILITY				
24	Are the firm's Financial Records publicly available?	☐	☐	
25	Has a Dun and Bradstreet report been reviewed?	☐	☐	
26	Is the award of this contract likely to create a burden on this firm's cashflow?	☐	☐	
27	Is the proposed teammate willing to contribute if an investment of corporate funds is necessary?	☐	☐	

		YES	NO	Notes
28	Are we expecting to require special marketing efforts of the proposed teammate? What and how much?	☐	☐	
TECHNICAL CAPABILITY / COMPETITION				
29	Is the win probability of been estimated? Is this the best opportunity for a likely award?	☐	☐	
30	Does this firm have required past performance experience?	☐	☐	
31	Does the firm employee a staff capable of successfully completing the SOW?	☐	☐	
32	If this is a set-aside procurement, is the SB prime capable of meeting the SBA requirements for Limitation on Subcontracting?	☐	☐	
REPUTATION				
33	Is the customer familiar with is firm?	☐	☐	
34	Do the firm have a positive relationship with key staff that are expected to have influence during contract performance?	☐	☐	
35	Does the firm have a positive reputation when acting as a prime contractor? Do they treat their subs fairly and with respect?	☐	☐	
36	Is a site visit necessary?	☐	☐	
37	Does the firm's website accurately reflect the firms standing within the Industry?	☐	☐	

		YES	NO	Notes
38	Has this firm filed a protest with the Government during the last 5 years? Was protest based on sound principles? What was the final outcome?	☐	☐	
39	Has this firm filed legal action against another contractor within last 5 years? Provide details for Sr Leadership review.	☐	☐	
40	Has this firm been the subject of legal actions filed by another contractor or customer within last 10 years? Provide details for Sr. Leadership review.	☐	☐	

Notes / Items for Consideration:

Appendix 3
Template for NDA

MUTUAL NON-DISCLOSURE AGREEMENT

This Agreement entered into as of [Insert Date] (hereafter referred to as the effective date), by and between **[Insert Full Legal Name of Party 1]** organized and existing under the laws of the State of [Insert Applicable State] and having its principal offices at [Insert Full Address for Party 1] (hereinafter called "**[Insert Name for Party 1]**") and **[Insert Full Legal Name of Party 2]**, organized and existing under the laws of the State of [Insert Applicable State], and having its principal office at [Insert Full Address for Party 2] (hereinafter called "**[Insert Name for Party 2]**")

WHEREAS, "**[Insert Name for Party 1]** and **[Insert Name for Party 2]** are desirous of exchanging proprietary information relating to "[Insert the name of solicitation or a descriptive name of the effort]" and hereafter referred to as the "Specific Purpose". The exchange of information considered company sensitive or proprietary is expected to be necessary for the parties to explore the likelihood of potential teaming in response to solicitation [Insert Government Solicitation Number].

WHEREAS, the parties desire to provide for a procedure whereby such proprietary information will be protected from unauthorized use and disclosure;

NOW, THEREFORE, in consideration of the foregoing and of the mutual promises contained herein, it is agreed as follows:

1. **Points of Contact:** In order for either party's Proprietary Information to be protected as described herein, it must be appropriately marked and submitted in written form as or if disclosures will include oral discloses or visually demonstrations (for example, software), a written summary of such disclosures that reasonably identifies the proprietary

information, and the marked written summary must be submitted to the following exclusive points of contact:

For [Insert Name for Party 1]:	**For** [Insert Name for Party 2]:
Insert POC Name	Insert POC Name
Insert Title of POC	Insert Title of POC
Insert Street Address	Insert Street Address
Insert City, State and Zip	Insert City, State and Zip
Phone:	Phone:
Email:	Email:

The above designated POCs are responsible for receiving all marked written declarations of protection, storing and safeguarding the information received, and managing compliance with all other provisions of this agreement.

Either party may change this point of contact by providing written notice to the other party. Delegation of responsibilities to any other individual without prior approval from both parties is strictly prohibited

2. **Definitions:** For the purposes of this Agreement:

    (a) The "Confidential Information" or "Proprietary Information" to be protected under the terms of this agreement shall include, but not be limited to, performance, sales, financial, contractual and special marketing information, ideas, technical data and concepts originated by the disclosing party, not previously

published or otherwise disclosed to the general public, not previously available without restriction to the receiving party or others, nor normally furnished to others without compensation, and which the disclosing party desires to protect against unrestricted disclosure or competitive use, and which is furnished pursuant to this Non-Disclosure Agreement and appropriately identified as being proprietary when furnished. "Proprietary Information", at the disclosure's discretion, may include both technical information and data and business and financial information.

(b) "Disclosing Party" refers to party making the disclosure of confidential or proprietary information and may be either of the parties that have executed this agreement.

(c) "Permitted Use" means the Confidential or Proprietary information may be used solely for the Specific Purpose of supporting the objectives identified in the preamble of this agreement, and for no other purpose.

(d) "Receiving Party" refers to the party receiving information from the disclosing party. Either of the parties that have executed this agreement may be the Receiving Party.

(e) "Responsible Party" means the Points of Contact for each party that is identified in Paragraph 1 of this agreement. These individuals are responsible for the protection, storing and safeguarding of all properly marked information they are provided, as well as the management and compliance with all provisions of this agreement.

3. **Recipient Obligations:** With respect to proprietary information so identified, both parties agree to the following:

(a) The recipient shall hold it in confidence from the date of receipt through the protection period

(b) The recipient shall use it only for information and evaluation purposes in connection with the specific program identified earlier in this document.

(c) The recipient shall make it available only to its employees having a "need to know" in order to carry out their respective functions in connection with the receiving party's effort on the Program.

(d) The recipient will NOT make any copy or excerpt of Proprietary Information without the disclosing party's prior written consent.

(e) The recipient shall not otherwise use or disclose any protected information to third parties without written authorization of the disclosing party. If the purpose of this agreement it to eventually submit a proposal to any branch or division of the US Government, the receiving party may disclose protected information to the US Government customer on a confidential basis provided the information bears the restrictive legend required by Federal Acquisition Regulation (FAR).

(f) Each party shall bear all costs and expenses incurred by it under or in connection with this Agreement. This Agreement is intended to provide only for the handling and protection of Proprietary Information. It shall not be construed as a Teaming, Joint Venture, Partnership, or other similar arrangement. Specifically, this Agreement shall not be construed in any manner to be an obligation to enter into a formal Teaming Agreement, contract or subcontract, nor shall it result in any claim for reimbursement of costs.

4. **Standards of Care:** The standard of care for protecting Proprietary Information imposed on the party receiving such information will be that degree of care (the same steps, methods

and precautions) the receiving party uses to prevent disclosure, acquisition, or use of its own Proprietary Information, but no less than a commercially reasonable standard of care.

Each party agrees that it shall protect the confidentiality of, and take all reasonable steps and precautions to prevent unauthorized disclosure, acquisition, or use of the Proprietary Information to prevent it from falling into the public domain or the public literature, or to prevent it from falling into the possession of unauthorized persons or entities. Neither party shall be liable for the inadvertent or accidental disclosure of Proprietary Information if such disclosure occurs despite the exercise of the same degree of care as such party normally takes to preserve its own such sensitive information or data, but no less than reasonable care

If either party loses or makes unauthorized disclosure of the other party's protected information, it shall notify such other party immediately, and in writing, of any misappropriation or misuse, by any person or entity, of Proprietary Information that comes to its attention or that it reasonably believes may have occurred at any time during the term of this Agreement. The party at fault shall take all steps reasonable and necessary to retrieve the lost or improperly disclosed information. Each party shall assume all legal liability for any breach of this Agreement by any of its 3rd party affiliates including any agents, consultants, representatives, subcontractors, vendors, and/or suppliers.

5. **Covered Information:** Protection of proprietary information will only be required when such information meets the following requirements:

   a) The information is provided in written format, and

   b) The information is clearly marked with an appropriate restrictive legend, and

    c) The information has been timely delivered to the Responsible Parties identified elsewhere in this agreement.

All other disclosures identified as proprietary at the time of disclosure (including visual, demonstrative, or verbal disclosures) shall be reduced to a written listing or summary and marked with an appropriate restrictive legend and delivered to the points of contact identified in Paragraph 1. Such assertions of required protection shall be received within three (3) working days after verbal disclosure or visual demonstration.

Neither party shall identify information as proprietary that is not in good faith believed to be proprietary, privileged, trade secret, company sensitive, or otherwise entitled to such protections or proprietary claims.

6. **Information Excluded from Protection:** Each party covenants and agrees that it will keep in confidence, and prevent the disclosure to any third party, or any person or persons outside its organization or to any unauthorized person, any and all information which is received from the disclosing party and has been protected in accordance with requirements of this agreement. Information shall not be afforded the protection of this Agreement from and after the first to occur of the following:

    a) was publicly available (in the public domain) at the time of disclosure, or

    b) when it is developed by the receiving party independently of the disclosing party, or

    c) when it is rightly obtained without restriction to the receiving party from a third party, or

    d) when it becomes publicly available other than through the fault or negligence of the receiving party, or

e) when it is released without restriction by the disclosing party to anyone, including the United States Government, or

f) when it is disclosed with the written approval of the other party, or

g) when it is disclosed pursuant to the provisions of a court order, or

h) The expiration of the mutually agreed period of protection.

The provisions of this Paragraph shall supersede the provisions of any inconsistent legend that may be affixed to said information by the disclosing party and the inconsistent provisions of any such legend shall be without any force or effect.

7. **Permitted Disclosure:** The Receiving Party may disclose Confidential Information under the following circumstances: (a) when required by applicable law, regulation, or court order, provided the Receiving Party gives prompt written notice to the Disclosing Party (unless prohibited by law) to allow for a protective order or other appropriate remedy; (b) to employees who require access to the Confidential Information for the purposes of performing obligations under this Agreement, provided such individuals are bound by written confidentiality obligations no less restrictive than those set forth herein; or (c) as necessary to comply with government audits, investigations, or regulatory submissions. The Receiving Party shall ensure that any permitted disclosures are limited to the minimum information necessary.

Neither party shall be liable for damages resulting from any disclosures of information pursuant to judicial action or Government regulations or for inadvertent disclosure thereof

where the customary degree of care has been exercised, provided that upon discovery of such inadvertent disclosure it shall have endeavored to correct the effects thereof and to prevent any further inadvertent disclosure

8. **Third-Party Disclosure Restrictions**: The Receiving Party shall not disclose the Disclosing Party's proprietary information to any affiliates, agents, subcontractors, representatives, consultants, auditors, or any other third parties without the prior written consent of the Disclosing Party. If such disclosure is permitted, the Receiving Party shall provide a written explanation detailing the necessity of access and the protective measures in place to safeguard the Disclosing Party's information. The Receiving Party must ensure that each third party has executed a separate NDA directly with the Disclosing Party prior to gaining access to any proprietary information. The Receiving Party agrees to accept full legal liability for any actions, breaches, or misuse of proprietary information by affiliates, agents, subcontractors, representatives, consultants, auditors, or third parties.

10. **Choice of Law**:   This Agreement and the performance thereof shall be governed by and construed in accordance with the laws of the County of [Insert Appropriate County], in The State of [Insert Appropriate State] excluding its conflicts of law provisions and including its statutes of limitations. The Parties hereby irrevocably consent to the exclusive jurisdiction of the federal and/or local courts in the State of [Insert Appropriate State] in connection with any action brought by either Party arising under or by reason of this Agreement. THE PARTIES HEREBY WAIVE TRIAL BY JURY WITH RESPECT TO ANY DISPUTE RELATING TO THIS AGREEMENT.

11. **Restricted Use:** The Receiving Party agrees that any proprietary information disclosed by the Disclosing Party under this

Agreement shall be used solely for the specific purpose stated elsewhere in this agreement. The Receiving Party shall not use the disclosed information for any other purpose, including but not limited to reverse engineering, deriving secondary data, or applying the information to unrelated programs or initiatives. By executing this agreement, the Receiving Party accepts full legal liability for any unauthorized use of the disclosed information, whether by itself or its employees, affiliates, consultants, agents, subcontractors or third parties. In the event of a breach, the rights of the parties to seek injunctive relief, monetary damages, and full indemnification for any losses incurred will be consistent with the clause entitled "Available Remedies". This clause shall survive the termination of this agreement.

12. **Rights in Data:** All technical data, software, and related deliverables developed or provided under this Agreement shall be subject to the following terms: (a) Proprietary data disclosed and marked as such shall remain the sole property of the Disclosing Party and shall not be disclosed or used by the Government except for purposes expressly authorized under this Agreement. (b) The Government shall have Government Purpose Rights to all data developed exclusively for this Agreement, allowing use, reproduction, and modification for government purposes only. (c) The disclosing Party shall provide all deliverables with appropriate data markings in compliance with FAR 52.227-14 and DFARS 252.227-7013. Any unmarked data shall be deemed to fall under Unlimited Rights. (d) Unauthorized use or disclosure of proprietary data shall entitle the Disclosing Party to injunctive relief, damages, and any other remedies available under applicable law.

13. **Term of Agreement**: The parties agree that the term of this Agreement shall commence on the effective date noted above and shall terminate three (3) years from that date. This period is considered the term of the agreement and is the period which proprietary information may be exchanged. Any extension of

this period must be agreed upon in writing by both parties prior to its expiration.

14. **Protection Period**: Regardless of the date information has been disclosed the recipient agrees to maintain, protect and prevent disclosure to unauthorized parties for a period of three (3) years following the last date of the term, or date of termination, of this Agreement. This additional two-year period is considered the protection period. During the protection period the receiving party shall safeguard and hold in strict confidence such proprietary Information and prevent disclosure thereof to third parties, without the written consent of the disclosing party. The receiving party shall further restrict the disclosure of such Proprietary Information to only those employees who have a need to know. During the above-mentioned protection period, no other use of the Proprietary Information is granted without the written consent of the Disclosing Party.

15. **Termination:** Either party may elect to terminate this agreement, at any time and for any reason, by providing the other party thirty (30) calendar days written Notice of Termination. However, the termination of this Agreement shall not relieve either party of their obligations hereunder regarding the protection and use of proprietary information disclosed hereunder prior to that date. Termination of this agreement does not alter in any way, the receiving party's obligations as addressed in the Survivability requirements addressed elsewhere in this agreement. Upon termination, the Recipient shall promptly return all documents and tangible materials representing the Disclosing Party's confidential information to the "Responsible Party" identified elsewhere in this agreement.

16. **Return of Proprietary Information:** At any time during the term of this agreement, or any specified protection period, the Disclosing party may provide a written request to the Receiving Party for return or destruction of all copies of any Proprietary

Contracts Classroom

Information of the Disclosing Party in the possession or control of the Receiving Party that was exchanged for the specific purpose identified in this agreement. The Receiving Party agrees to provide a full, complete, and timely response to the Disclosing Parties request within five (5) business days of receiving such request. Any time one party elects, or is required, to destroy the other parties protected information, the party performing such destruction shall send the other party a written notice of destruction which has been duly certified by an appropriate representative of the party. However, the Receiving Party may keep one copy for auditing and records purposes only and such copy shall be held to the obligations in this Agreement in perpetuity.

If the Purpose of this Agreement includes the submission of a proposal by one of the Parties which would incorporate Proprietary Information of the other Party, then the receiving Party may retain copies of the proposal for its internal use, including the Proprietary Information of the disclosing Party, provided that no use may be made of the Proprietary Information other than for the stated Purpose of this Agreement. The Parties understand that copies of such proposals may be retained by customers to whom they were submitted.

17. **Export Control**: This Agreement does not authorize export of technical data. The Receiving Party represents and warrants that no technical data furnished to it by the Disclosing Party shall be disclosed to any foreign national, nation, firm, or country, including foreign nationals employed by or associated with the Receiving Party, nor shall any technical data be exported from the United States without first complying with all U.S. export control regulations including the requirements of the International Traffic in Arms Regulations (ITAR) or the Export Administration Regulations (EAR), including the requirement for obtaining any export license if applicable. The Receiving Party shall first obtain the written consent of the Disclosing

Party prior to submitting any re-quest for authority to export any such technical data. The Receiving Party shall indemnify and hold the Disclosing Party harmless for all claims, demands, damages, costs, fines, penalties, attorney's fees, and all other expenses arising from failure of the Receiving Party to comply with this clause or the ITAR and EAR.

18. **Notice of Breach:** The Receiving Party shall promptly notify the Disclosing Party in writing of any unauthorized disclosure, loss, or suspected breach of Confidential Information, no later than five (5) business days from the date the breach is discovered. Such notice shall include a description of the breach, the date it occurred, the actions taken to contain or mitigate the breach, and any additional details reasonably requested by the Disclosing Party. The Receiving Party shall cooperate fully with the Disclosing Party to investigate the breach, mitigate any harm, and prevent further unauthorized disclosures. Failure to provide timely notice shall be deemed a material breach of this Agreement, entitling the Disclosing Party to all available legal and equitable remedies.

19. **Available Remedies:** Both parties acknowledge that unauthorized use or disclosure of the Proprietary Information could cause irreparable harm and significant injury to the other party, for which monetary damages may not be a sufficient remedy. Accordingly, any controversy, dispute, or claim arising out of or related to this Agreement, including any breach thereof and issues that cannot be resolved thru mutual negotiation, shall be resolved through litigation. Both parties agree that the non-breaching party shall be entitled, without waiving any other rights or remedies, to seek, without bond, equitable relief, including injunctions, to prevent unauthorized use or disclosure of Proprietary Information. Provided that the court finds that a breach occurred, the breaching party shall be liable and shall pay to the non-breaching party all reasonable costs and fees, including, but not limited to, attorney's fees and

court costs, incurred by such non-breaching party in connection with such litigation, including any appeal therefrom. This clause shall survive termination of the Agreement.

20. **Warranty:** The Disclosing Party makes no representations or warranties, express or implied, as to the accuracy, completeness, adequacy, sufficiency, or freedom from defect of any kind, including freedom from any patent infringement that may result from the use of such Proprietary Information provided under this Agreement. All information is provided "AS IS" and without any warranties of merchantability or fitness for a particular purpose. Neither Party shall incur any liability or obligation whatsoever by reason of such information. The Receiving Party acknowledges that the Disclosing Party shall have no liability arising from the use, reliance, or interpretation of the Proprietary Information by the Receiving Party or any third party.

21. **Assignment:** Neither party may assign or transfer this Agreement, or any rights and obligations hereunder, to any third party without the prior written consent of the other party, which consent shall not unreasonably be withheld. Any consent request not responded to within ten (10) calendar days shall be determined to be acceptable and agreed to by all parties. This consent requirement shall not apply in the event either party shall change its corporate name. Any attempted assignment in violation of this provision shall be null and void. This Agreement shall be binding upon and inure to the benefit of the parties and their respective successors and permitted assigns.

22. **Change of Control:** In the event of a Change of Control of either party, the party experiencing the Change of Control ("Affected Party") shall provide an advance written notification to the other party, no less than forty-five [45] calendar days before the Change of Control occurs. For the purposes of this Agreement, "Change of Control" shall mean a transaction or series of transactions resulting in:

a) the sale, transfer, or assignment of more than fifty percent (50%) of the Affected Party's ownership interests;

b) the merger, consolidation, or reorganization of the Affected Party with another entity that results in a change in the party's controlling interest; or

c) the sale, transfer, or assignment of all or substantially all of the Affected Party's assets.

Upon receipt of notice of a Change of Control, the other party may, at its sole discretion:

1) Terminate this Agreement with a ten (10) Calendar days' written notice if the Change of Control involves a transfer to a competitor or entity adverse to the terminating party's interests; or

2) Require the Affected Party or its successor entity to reaffirm in writing its obligations under this Agreement within five (5) business days of notice.

The confidentiality and non-use obligations of this Agreement shall survive any Change of Control and bind any successor or assign of the Affected Party.

23. **No Implied License:** Nothing contained in this Agreement shall be construed as granting, by implication, estoppel, or otherwise, any license or rights under any patents, copyrights, trade secrets, trademarks, or other intellectual property of the Disclosing Party. The Proprietary Information provided shall only be used for the purposes expressly permitted by this Agreement and shall not be reproduced, modified, reverse-engineered, or incorporated into any products or services without the prior written consent of the Disclosing Party.

Further, nothing contained in this Non Disclosure Agreement shall grant to either party any right, title, interest, or license in, or to, the inventions, patents, technical data, computer software, or software documentation of the other party.

Nothing contained in this Non-Disclosure Agreement shall grant to either party the right to make commitments of any kind for or on behalf of any other party without the prior written consent of that other party.

24. **Severability:** If any provision, provision title, or the application of any aspect thereof, or any portion of this Agreement are held to be unenforceable, illegal, or void by a court of competent jurisdiction, for any reason whatsoever, the remaining provisions hereof shall nevertheless remain enforceable, and the court making such determination shall modify the provisions hereof held to be unenforceable so as to preserve the enforceability of this Agreement to the maximum extent permitted by applicable law. The failure of either party to enforce any provision contained herein shall not be deemed a waiver of any other provision contained herein.

25. **Survivable Terms:** Unless otherwise stated within this document, the obligations of the parties under Paragraphs 2. – Definitions; 3. – Covered Information; 4. – Recipient Obligations; 9. – Standards of Care; 10. - Choice of Law; 11.- Restriced Use; 14.- Protection Period; 15-Termination; 16. - Return of Proprietary Information 19. – Available Remedies; and 25. - Severability; will survive the termination or expiration of this Agreement. Upon termination, the receiving party will promptly return all confidential information of the disclosing party in its possession, custody, or control, including all copies and derivatives thereof.

26. **Entire Agreement:** This Agreement embodies all the understandings between the Parties concerning the subject matter of this Agreement. This Agreement merges all prior

discussions and writings between the parties as to confidentiality of information related to the subject. No other unwritten or implied terms exist. Neither of the parties shall be bound by any conditions, warranties, or representations with respect to confidentiality of information other than as expressly provided in this Agreement, or as set forth in a subsequent written amendment signed by the parties.

IN WITNESS WHEREOF, the parties have caused this Agreement to be duly executed in duplicate originals by their duly authorized representatives.

Insert Name for Party 1　　　　　　**Insert Name for Party 2**

_____　　_____
Signature　　　　　　　　　　　　　Signature

_____　　_____
Title　　　　　　　　　　　　　　　Title

_____　　_____
Date　　　　　　　　　　　　　　　Date

Contracts Classroom

Afterword

Congratulations on completing *Become a Government Contracting Wizard: Mastering NDAs for Government Contractors*. You've taken a significant step toward not only mastering Non-Disclosure Agreements but also enhancing your career in the competitive world of government contracting. NDAs may seem like small pieces of the larger contracting puzzle, but as you've learned, they play a critical role in protecting your company's interests, building trust, and setting the foundation for successful partnerships.

This journey has equipped you with the tools, insights, and strategies to approach NDAs with confidence and precision. You've gained the ability to assess risks, negotiate critical terms, and ensure compliance with both legal standards and best practices. More importantly, you've positioned yourself as a trusted expert—someone your organization can rely on to handle sensitive information and navigate the complexities of government contracting with skill and professionalism.

But this isn't the end—it's the beginning of your continued growth as a NDA wizard. The knowledge you've gained here will serve as a foundation for your future success, but the contracting environment is always evolving. Regulations change, industry practices shift, and new challenges emerge. Stay curious, stay informed, and keep refining your expertise. Revisit the principles and examples in this book as needed, and don't hesitate to adapt them to meet the demands of new situations.

Remember, being a NDA wizard is about more than just technical knowledge—it's about fostering trust, protecting value, and ensuring that every agreement you handle reflects the professionalism and precision you bring to your work.

As you move forward, I hope this book has not only demystified NDAs but also inspired you to approach them with the confidence and mastery that sets you apart. Whether you're leading negotiations, mentoring colleagues, or managing complex agreements, know that you have the skills to succeed and the foundation to excel.

Thank you for taking this journey with me. Now, go forth and wield your newfound expertise with confidence. You are the NDA Wizard. Protect your company's interests. Advance your career. And, most importantly, continue to make a difference in the world of government contracting.

Tim Magnusson, CPCM
Author, *Become a Government Contracting Wizard: Mastering NDAs for Government Contractors*

About the Author

Tim Magnusson, CPCM
Author

Tim's professional career has been devoted to the Government contracting profession supporting all federal service branches in multiple types of business sizes, classifications, and categories.

He is a recognized subject matter expert in government contracting and acquisition management. His skill set includes the possession of a keen business acumen, skilled negotiator, and an in-depth knowledge of highly technical clauses and provisions.

Tim is the founder of ContractsClassroom.com, where he and his team deliver comprehensive government contracting education through online courses, webinars, and special event presentations. In addition to his work with ContractsClassroom.com, Tim serves as a senior leader in the contracting profession with a highly respected defense contractor.

In addition to a Master of Science in Management degree from Florida Institute of Technology and a Bachelor's Degree in Communication from The University of Alabama, Tim holds the Certified Professional Contracts Manager (CPCM) designation from the National Contract Management Association (NCMA) reflecting his knowledge of all facets of contract management within the government and commercial sectors.

www.ingramcontent.com/pod-product-compliance
Lightning Source LLC
Chambersburg PA
CBHW070614030426
42337CB00020B/3801